MYSTERY OF THE UNIVERSE

MYSTERY OF THE UNIVERSE

The Human Being, Image of Creation

Sixteen lectures given in Dornach, Switzerland, between 9 April and 16 May 1920

RUDOLF STEINER

RUDOLF STEINER PRESS
LONDON

Translated by George and Mary Adams. Revised by
Matthew Barton

Rudolf Steiner Press
51 Queen Caroline Street
London W6 9QL

www.rudolfsteinerpress.com

Published by Rudolf Steiner Press 2001

First published in English as *Man: Hieroglyph of the Universe* by Rudolf
Steiner Press 1972

Originally published in German under the title *Entsprechungen zwischen
Mikrokosmos und Makrokosmos, Der Mensch—eine Hieroglyphe des Weltenalls*
(volume 201 in the *Rudolf Steiner Gesamtausgabe* or Collected Works) by
Rudolf Steiner Verlag, Dornach. This authorized translation is published
by kind permission of the Rudolf Steiner Nachlassverwaltung, Dornach

Translation © Rudolf Steiner Press 2001

A catalogue record for this book is available from the British Library

ISBN 1 85584 069 3

Cover illustration by Anne Stockton. Cover design by Andrew Morgan
Typeset by DP Photosetting, Aylesbury, Bucks.
Printed and bound in Great Britain by Cromwell Press Limited,
Trowbridge, Wilts.

Contents

Introduction

This series of lectures rates among the most significant and profound that Rudolf Steiner ever gave. It ranks in terms of reader enlivenment—exhilaration even—with *Harmony of the Creative Word*, representing as it does a veritable score for the Music of the Spheres and the harmonies of the heavenly choirs. At the same time it sets out with mathematical exactness the astronomical and other relevant details which reveal the structures that sustain the entire universe. Here is genuine harmony between spiritual science proper and a material science shorn of misconceptions and misinterpretations of the facts. These findings bear Steiner's unique stamp of transparent authenticity and crystal clarity. Once, twice or even thrice read, it will not fail to enthral.

The original title for it, *Kosmologische Betrachtungen*, is translatable into English as *Cosmological Reflections*, which hints at something of a play on words, for they not only call for earnest contemplation in terms of close application and study in view of their penetratingly thought-provoking character, but also refer to the complementary relationships between the human being as microcosm and the universe as macrocosm in a straightforwardly literal manner. Their very importance may well give reason for the fact that these 16 lectures were delivered over a period of six successive weekends, thus providing optimal opportunity for individuals to attend them.

They discuss in broad as well as particular terms the significance of the various dimensions within the natural order, and the relations of human beings, animals and plants with directions in space. Set out in fine detail are the various rhythmical rotatory, orbital and other gestures of the celestial bodies, and how these are reflected in the various life-forms to be found on the earth, particularly where the complexities of human nature and existence are concerned. In all the revelations and insights that Rudolf Steiner gives in these lectures, the rules of scientific investigation and presentation are clearly discernible, as are the laws and principles which must feature in all types of systematic enquiry.

The main theme pervading throughout may be expressed in his often reiterated statement that human beings can find absolutely nothing in the universe unless they find it in themselves first, and vice versa. Every part has its counterpart and every poise its counterpoise, for absolute balance must be maintained. Again and again Steiner echoes the Hermetic maxim 'As above, so below; as below, so above', which he further augments with 'As within, so without; as without, so within'. These concepts, which he deals with convincingly, are based on the demonstrable fact that at all times and in all circumstances spirit is anterior to matter, and matter posterior to spirit. In other words, spirit is unremittingly and without exception the dynamic agent to which matter is passively patient, which fundamental law is applicable within both realms.

Steiner averred that anthroposophy is rooted in cosmosophy, and has developed out of it; hence it must be so that knowledge of the one is knowledge of the other. Therefore, as human beings are primarily spiritual in nature, and only secondarily beings of matter, there can be no incompatibilities or disparities. In reality, we are not children of the earth but children of the heavens; we have descended from and been fashioned by cosmic powers, and made manifest from the earth beneath our feet. In overall terms, we are mere sojourners on the earth, which represents a lodging rather than a home.

★

These lectures of Rudolf Steiner have, in typically straight-forward fashion, enriched *material* as well as *spiritual* science. He has made an exceptionally important contribution to our appreciation of the fact that law and order rule in both the heavenly spiritual and earthly material worlds. The Greek word *kosmos* can mean not only 'world' or 'universe'—and this directly on account of its 'perfect arrangement'—but also 'order' as antithetic to 'chaos'. Moreover, since the laws and ordinances of the creative spiritual powers are utterly moral, it follows that natural laws must likewise show consistency and uniformity, and lack any tendency to 'lie' or deviate to any significant extent. Everything, whether material and manifest or spiritual and unmanifest must, in terms of the Whole, be co-existent, parallel and complementary.

We should always bear in mind Steiner's assertion that humanity truly belongs to the spiritual hierarchies, as the tenth, as Spirits of Love and Freedom. During our early stages of evolution we existed under the auspices of these exalted beings, having no choice but to accept circumstances as they were at any one time. We human beings, alone among the higher hierarchies from whom we have descended, are gradually maturing, however distant the goal, towards the accomplishment of our own impulses, fulfilment of our own destiny, and attainment of our own ideals. Stage by stage, we have as microcosms evolved from out of the macrocosm, from the time when the Gods thought and willed in us to that when we acquired an intelligence and free will of our own. For this to come about the severing of links with our divine origins in the purely spiritual realms was inevitable. In effect, human consciousness has evolved from a state of extensive appre-hension of the spiritual world combined with limited aware-ness of the material world to limited awareness of the supersensible world but extensive understanding of the material world. During this lengthy process we acquired our present individual intelligence and free will.

However, living as we do in a world that has necessarily become materialistic through and through, we find ourselves participants in Archangel Michael's battle against retrogressive powers and devices. In so many areas of science, including cosmogony and evolution, orthodoxy rules. We have surrounded ourselves with mechanical contrivances of every kind, particularly electronic apparatus which belong to the 'sub-natural' realms, and which have become an indispensable part of modern life. Moreover, information technology is evolving from the status of servant to that of master. How easy it is to be taken in by simulated 'virtual reality' television programmes, and to hear in the name of science, instead of tentative or provisional propositions being offered for consideration, seemingly unchallengeable and unarguable statements and assertions being confidently and persuasively presented, complete with impressive 'visual aids', by experts exuding self-assurance and aplomb. Irritating as this kind of presumptuousness may be for many people, students of spiritual science have a virtually impossible task in refuting whatever notions, of various degrees of feasibility, proffered so blatantly as fact by such 'authorities'.

Rudolf Steiner asserted that the study of natural science outside mankind must be underpinned by an understanding of human nature. It is self-evident that complete harmony between these two principles must obtain, for their inception is easily traceable to a common source. But all materialists are isolationists, for it is their trade to compartmentalize everything, to deal in analysis rather than synthesis, parts rather than wholes. There are of course many points of contact between material science and spiritual science, and a good example of this, and of particular interest to many people, especially in our outer-space-conscious times, and one which is relevant within the present context, is that of the lemniscatory passage of our whole solar system through cosmic space. These lectures deal with this important topic at some length, and it may well be that the time is ripe for bringing the whole matter to the attention of contemporary scientists and other interested thinkers in vigorous and authoritative terms. During the conference with teachers of the first Steiner Waldorf School in Stuttgart on 25 September 1919 this matter was brought up and discussed. Rudolf Steiner observed that if the third law of Copernicus was invoked as well as the first two, 'it would be child's play to show up today's teaching as humbug'.

Be that as it may, he affirmed that there is indeed light at the end of the materialist tunnel, arguing that sooner or later orthodox scientists will be faced with riddles that can only be solved by taking the spiritual into account. Steiner repeatedly emphasized that supersensibly acquired knowledge is in complete and necessary agreement with that gained from the world of the senses. This cannot be otherwise; if to the 'half-reality' of sense-perception is added the complementary 'half-reality' of supersensible perception, the result can only be the apprehension of complete and absolute reality.

Gilbert Childs
April 2001

Lecture 1

Today I shall try to give a wider view of a subject already often touched upon. I have frequently pointed out how moral and intellectual conceptions diverge for modern man. On the one hand we are brought, through intellectual thinking, to recognition of the iron necessity of nature. In accordance with this necessity we see everything in *nature* under the law of cause and effect. And we ask also, when *man* performs an action: what has caused it, what is the inner or outer cause? This recognition of the inevitable necessity of all that occurs has in modern times acquired a more scientific character. In earlier times it had a more theological character, and still has for many people. It takes on a scientific character when we believe that what we do is dependent on our bodily constitution and on the influences that work upon it. There are still many people who think that man acts just as inevitably as a stone falls to the ground. There you have the natural scientific colouring of the necessity concept. The view of those more inclined to theology might be described as follows: everything is pre-ordained by some kind of divine power or providence and man must carry out what is predestined by that divine power. Thus on the one hand we have the necessity of natural science, and on the other absolute divine prescience. In neither case can one speak of human freedom at all.

Over against this stands the whole *moral* world. Man feels of this world that he cannot so much as speak of it without postulating free will; for if he has no possibility of free voluntary choice, he cannot speak of a morality of human action. He does however feel responsibility, he feels moral impulses; he must therefore recognize a moral world. I have mentioned before how the impossibility of building a bridge between the two, between the world of necessity and the world of morals, led Kant to write two critiques, the *Critique of Pure Reason* in which he applies himself to investigating the nature of simple necessity, and the *Critique of Applied Reason* in which he enquires into what belongs to the moral universe. Then he felt compelled to write also a *Critique of Judgment* which was intended as an intermediary between the two, but which ended in being no more than a compromise, and approached reality only when it turned to the world of *beauty*, the world of artistic creation. This goes to show how we have the world of necessity on the one hand and on the other the world of free moral action, but cannot find anything to unite the two except the world of artistic semblance, where—let us say, in sculpture or in painting—we appear to be picturing what comes from natural necessity, but impart to it something which is free from necessity, thus giving it the appearance of being *free in necessity*.

The truth is that we are unable to build a bridge between the world of necessity and the world of freedom unless we find the way through spiritual science. Spiritual science, however, can only be developed by fulfilling the aphorism which won respect centuries ago, the Greek saying of Apollo: 'Know thyself!' Now this admonition, which does not mean burrowing into one's own subjectivity but implies a knowledge of the whole being of man and the position he occupies in the universe, is a search that must find a place in our whole spiritual movement, through spiritual science.

From this point of view we may really say that our anthroposophical spiritual movement has in the last few days begun to show clearly to the spiritual life of humanity how we must seek to illuminate and imbue modern thinking with a knowledge of man; for it is a fact that this knowledge of man has largely been lost in modern times. This was our aim in the course of lectures that has just been held for doctors, where an initial attempt was made to throw positive light upon matters with which medical science has to concern itself.* In the series of lectures given by our friends and myself, we tried to show the right relationship between the individual sciences and what they can receive from spiritual science. It would be very good indeed for a strong consciousness of the need for such attempts to live within our movement; for if we are to succeed it is absolutely necessary to make clear to the outer world—in a sense, to compel it to understand—that here no kind of superficiality prevails in any domain, but rather an earnest striving for real knowledge. This is often prevented by the way in which things reach the public from our own circles, so that it is supposed, or may easily be maliciously suggested, that all kinds of sectarianism and dilettantism are at work here. It is for us to increasingly convince the outer world how earnest is the striving underlying all that this building represents. Such attempts as we made over the last few weeks must be carried further by the forces of the whole anthroposophical movement; for we have now made a beginning with a true knowledge of man which must form the foundation of all true spiritual culture. It is true to say that from the middle of the fifteenth century man's previous concrete relation to the world has been growing more and more filtered, one may say, and abstract. In olden times, through atavistic clairvoyance man knew much more of himself than he does today, for since the middle of the [nineteenth] century intellectualism has spread over the whole of the so-called civilized world. Intellectualism is based upon a very small part of man's being; and it produces accordingly no more than an abstract schema of knowledge about the world.

---

* Published as *Introducing Anthroposophical Medicine*, Anthroposophic Press, New York, 1999.

What has knowledge of the world become in the course of the last centuries? In its relation to the universe, it has become mere mathematical-mechanical calculation, to which in recent times have been added the results of spectral analysis; these again are purely physical, and within the physical domain purely mechanical-mathematical. Astronomy observes the courses of the stars and calculates; but it notices only those forces which show the universe, in so far as the earth is enclosed in it, as a great machine, a great mechanism. It is true to say that this mechanical-mathematical method of observation has come to be regarded as the only one that can actually lead to real knowledge.

Now what does the mentality, which finds expression in this mathematical-mechanical construction of the universe, rely upon? It reckons with something that is founded to some extent in the nature of man, but only in a very small part of him. It reckons first with the abstract *three dimensions of space*. Astronomy reckons with the abstract three dimensions of space; it distinguishes *one* dimension, a *second* (drawing on blackboard) and a *third*, at right angles. It fixes attention on a star in movement, or on the position of a star, by looking at these three dimensions of space. Now man would be unable to speak of three-dimensional space if he had not experienced it in his own being. Man *experiences* three-dimensional space. In the course of his life he experiences first the vertical dimension. As a child he crawls, and then he raises himself upright and thus experiences the vertical dimension. It would not be possible for man to speak of the vertical dimension if he did not experience it. To think that he could find anything in the universe other than he finds in himself would be an illusion. Man finds this vertical dimension only by experiencing it himself. By stretching out our hands and arms at right angles to the vertical we obtain the second dimension. In what we experience when breathing or speaking, in the inhaling and exhaling of the air, or in what we experience when we eat, when the food in the body moves from front to back, we experience the third dimension. Only because man experiences these three dimensions within him does he project them into external space. Man can find absolutely nothing in the universe unless he finds it first in himself. The strange thing is that in this age of abstractions, which began in the middle of the fifteenth century, man has given all three dimensions a similar quality. That is, he has simply left out of his thought the concrete distinction between them. He has left out what makes the three dimensions different to him. If he were to express his real human *experience*, he would say: My vertical, my encompassing or my out-stretching dimension. He would have to assume a difference in *quality* between the three spatial dimensions. Were he to do this, he would no longer be able to conceive of an astronomical cosmogony in the present abstract way. He would obtain a less purely intellectual cosmic picture. For this, however, he would have to experience in a more concrete way his own relationship to the three dimensions. Today he has no such experience. He does not experience, for instance, the quality of the upright position, of being vertical; and so he is not aware that he is in a vertical position for the simple reason that he *moves together with the earth* in a certain direction which adheres to the vertical. Neither does he know that he makes his breathing movements, his digestive and eating movements as well as other movements, in a direction through which the earth also moves. All this adherence to certain directions of movement implies an adaptation, a fitting into, the movements of the universe. Today man takes no account whatever of this concrete understanding of the dimensions; hence he cannot define his position in the great cosmic process. He does not know how he stands in it, nor that he is as it were a part and member of it. We will increasingly have to take steps to obtain a knowledge of man, a self-knowledge, and so a knowledge of our place in the universe.

The three dimensions have really become so abstract for man that he would find it extremely difficult to train himself to feel that by living in them he is taking part in certain movements of the earth and the planetary system. A spiritual-scientific method of thought however can be applied to our knowledge of man by beginning to seek an understanding of the three dimensions. It is difficult to attain; but we shall more easily raise ourselves to this spatial knowledge of man if we consider, not the three lines of space at right angles, but three *planes*. Consider the following for a moment. We shall readily perceive that our *symmetry* has something to do with our *thinking*. We can discover an elementary natural gesture that we make to express a process of thinking and judgement. When we place finger on nose and move through this plane here (*a drawing is made*), we are moving through the vertical symmetry plane which divides our left side from our right. This plane passing through the nose and through the whole body is the plane of symmetry, and we can become conscious that it is connected with all the discriminating that goes on within us, all the thinking and judging that discriminates and divides. Starting from this elementary gesture, it is actually possible to become aware of how all human functions are related to this plane.

Consider the function of seeing. We see with two eyes, in such a way that the lines of vision intersect. We see a point with two eyes; but we see it as one point because the lines of sight cross each other. Much of our human activity is so regulated that our understanding and grasping of things is connected with this plane.

We can then turn to another plane which would pass through the heart and divide man back from front. In front, man is physiognomically organized, so as to express his soul being. This physiognomical-soul structure is divided off by a plane which stands at right angles to the first. As our right and left is divided by a plane, so too is our front divided from our back. We need only stretch out our arms, our hands, directing the physiognomical part of the hand (in contrast to the merely organic part) forwards and the organic part of the hands backwards, and then imagine a plane through the principal lines which thus arise, and we obtain the plane I mean.

In like manner we can locate a third plane which would mark off all that is contained in head and countenance from what is organized below into body and limbs. Thus we should obtain a third plane which again is at right angles to the other two.

One can acquire a feeling for these three planes. How the feeling for the first is obtained has already been shown; it is to be felt as the plane of discriminative *thinking*. The second plane, which divides man into front and back (anterior and posterior), would be precisely what reveals man as *man*, for this plane cannot be delineated in the same way in the animal. The symmetry plane can be drawn in the animal but not the vertical plane. This second (vertical) plane would be connected with everything pertaining to human *will*. The third, the horizontal, would be connected with everything pertaining to human *feeling*. Let us try once more to get an idea of these dimensions through their elementary gestures, and we shall see that this can help further our understanding.

Everything through which we bring our feelings to expression, whether it be a feeling of greeting or one of thankfulness or any other form of sympathetic feeling, is in a way connected with the horizontal plane. So too we can see that in a sense we must relate the will to the vertical plane. It is possible to acquire a feeling for these three planes. Once we have done this, we will be obliged to form our conception of the universe according to these three planes—just as we would, if we only regarded the three dimensions of space in an abstract way, be obliged to calculate in the mechanical-mathematical way in which Galileo or Copernicus calculated movements and positions in the universe. Real relationships in this universe will then reveal themselves to us. We will no longer merely calculate according to the three dimensions of space; but once we have learnt to feel these three planes, we will notice that there is a difference between right and left, over and under, back and front. In mathematics it is a matter of indifference whether some object is a little further right or left, or before or behind. If we *simply measure*, we measure below or above, we measure right or left or we measure forward or backward. In whatever position three metres is set, it remains three metres. At most we distinguish, in order to pass from position to movement, the dimensions at right angles to one another. This we do, however, only because we cannot make do with simple measurement alone, for then our world would shrink to no more than a straight line. If however, we learn to embody thinking, feeling and willing in these three planes in a real, concrete way, and to place ourselves as soul-spiritual beings, with our thinking, feeling and willing, into spatial dimensions—then just as we learn to apply to astronomy the three abstract dimensions of space, so do we also learn to apply to it the threefold division of man as a being of soul and spirit. And it becomes possible if we have here (*drawing*) Saturn, Jupiter, Mars, Sun, Venus, Mercury and lastly Earth, then it becomes possible, if we look at the sun, to observe it in its outer manifestation as something separating, as a dividing element. We must think of a horizontal plane passing through the sun, and we shall no longer regard what is above the plane and what is below as merely quantitative, but must regard the plane as a dividing plane and distinguish the planets as being above or below. Thus we shall no longer say: Mars is so many miles distant from the sun, Venus so many miles; but we shall learn to apply knowledge of man to our knowledge of the universe, and say: It is no mere question of abstract dimensions to see that the human head or the nose is at such and such a distance from the horizontal plane which I have called the plane of feeling, and the heart at such and such a distance; but I shall bring their position and distance above and below into connection with their formation and structure. So too I shall no longer say of Mars and Mercury that the one is at such a distance and the other at such another distance from the sun, but I shall know that if I regard the sun as a dividing partition, Mars being above must be of one nature and Mercury being below of another.

I shall now be able to place a similar plane perpendicularly through the sun. Thus the movements of Jupiter, let us say, or of Mars, will be such that at one time it will stand on the right of this plane and then go across it and stand on the left. If I simply proceed abstractly, according to dimensions, I shall find it is sometimes on the right and sometimes on the left, and such and such a number of miles. But if I study cosmic space concretely, as I must study my own being, it is not a matter of indifference whether a planet is sometimes on the left and at other times on the right. I can say that there is the *same kind of difference* whether it is on the right or left as there is between a left and right organ. It is not sufficient to say that the liver is so many centimetres to the right of the symmetrical axis, the stomach so many centimetres to the left, for the two are dissimilar in formation *because* the one is a right organ and the other a left. It is actually the case that Jupiter becomes different according to whether it is on the right or the left— even to the naked eye.

In the same way I might make a third plane, and would again have to form a judgement in accordance with that. And if I extend my knowledge of man to the universe, I shall be obliged, as I connected the one plane with human thinking, and the second plane with human feeling, to consider the third plane as connected with human will.

By describing all this I only wanted to show how modern astronomy has no more than a last, extremely abstract vestige of concrete knowledge when it speaks of the three planes perpendicular to one another, to which the positions and movements of the stars are quite accidentally related; and when it then makes mechanical calculations about the whole universe according to these positions. In the astronomical conception of Galileo, only this one thing is taken into consideration for the universe—*abstract space*, with its point relationships. This knowledge can however be enlarged to become an active and powerful knowledge of man. One can say: Man is a thinking, feeling and willing being. As an outward, spatial being, his thinking relates to one plane, his willing to another at right angles with it, and his feeling to a third at right angles to both. This must apply also in the external world. Since the middle of the fifteenth century, man has really known no more than that he extends in three abstract dimensions; all else is just observations based on that. A true knowledge of man must be regained, and thereby also a knowledge of the cosmos. Then man will understand how necessity and free will are related, and how *both* can apply to man, since he is born from the cosmos. Naturally if one only takes this last abstract vestige of the human being's true nature—the three abstract dimensions at right angles to one another—if that is all one wants to imagine, then the universe appears terribly impoverished. Poor, infinitely impoverished is our present astronomical view of the universe; and it will not become richer until we press forward to a real knowledge of man, until we really learn to look into man's true nature.

The anthroposophical world view includes matter, the material, as part of real spiritual knowledge. Do not such things as thinking, feeling and willing appear to human knowledge as terribly bare abstractions nowadays? Man does not investigate himself thoroughly enough. He does not ask himself about the true nature of what these words designate. A great deal has become mere phrase. One should really ask oneself conscientiously, when using the word thinking, whether it presents any clear idea—not to speak of feeling and willing. But our speech becomes clear and plain the moment we pass from the mere making of phrases, the using of lofty words, and go back to *pictures*; even when we take just that one picture for thinking—putting the finger to the side of the nose! We do not need to do it always, but we know that this gesture is often naturally made when we have to think hard, just as we point the finger to the chin when we want to indicate we are contemplating something or paying attention! We enter this plane precisely because we wish to form judgements there about something relating to us. We bisect our organism as it were into right and left; for we really act quite differently with our right and left sense-organs. This we can appreciate if we observe that we use the left sense-organs to sense outer objects; and in our thinking too, there is a sort of handling or feeling of external objects. With the right sense-organs we 'sense our sense' of them, as it were. It is then that they first become our own. We could never have attained a sense of ego or self if we were not able to bring together our perceptions of what we experience on the right with what we experience on the left. By simply laying our hands one over the other we have a picture of the ego-concept. It is indeed true that by beginning to use clear images instead of mere phraseology, man will become inwardly richer and will gain the faculty of visualizing the universe in richer detail.

By taking this path we shall find that the universe comes to life again for us, and that we human beings share in its life. Then we shall learn again how to build a bridge between universe and man. When this is done man will be able to perceive whether there is in the universe an impulse of natural necessity for *all* that is in man, wholly determining us, or whether the universe in some measure leaves us free. As long as we live in abstractions, we cannot build a bridge between moral and natural law. We must be able to ask ourselves how far natural law extends in the universe, and where something enters in which we *cannot include* under the aspect of natural law. Then we uncover a relationship which has its significance for man too, a relationship between what comes under natural law and what is free and moral. In this way we learn to connect a meaning with the statement: 'Mars is a planet far from the sun, Venus a planet nearer the sun.' By simply stating their distances in abstract numbers we have said nothing or at least very little, for to define things in this way, according to the methods of modern astronomy, is equivalent to saying: I look at the line which passes through man's two arms and hands, and I speak of an organ that is 2½ decimetres from this line. Now this organ may be a certain distance under the line, and another organ a certain distance above it; it is not, however, the *distance* that makes the difference, but the fact that one organ is *above* and the other *below*. Were there no difference between above and below, there would be no difference between the nose or eyes and the stomach! The eyes are only eyes because they are above, and the stomach is only a stomach because it is below this line. The inner nature of the organ is conditioned by the position.

Similarly the inner nature of Mars is qualified by its position *outside* the sun's orbit, and that of Venus by its position *within* the sun's orbit. If one does not understand the essential difference between an organ in the human head and an organ in the human trunk—the one lying over and the other under this line—then one cannot know that Mars and Venus, or Mars and Mercury are essentially different. The ability to think of the universe as an organism depends on our learning to understand the living image of the organism we have before us. We must learn to perceive man as a living image of the universe, for he gives us the opportunity of seeing at first hand how different are above and below, left and right, before and behind. We must learn this first in man, and we shall then find it in the universe.

The modern view of the universe held by natural science really gives a world picture omitting man—recognizing him only as the highest of the animals, that is to say an abstraction.

Man is not included in it at all, and therefore the universe appears to this world view as a mathematical picture only, in which the universal origin of freedom and morality can never be recognized. It is, however, of the utmost importance that we learn to perceive scientifically the connection between moral law and natural necessity. Today I have endeavoured to show you, in perhaps rather subtle concepts, how a knowledge of the universe is to be gained from a knowledge of man.

I was able to show the doctors, in a strictly scientific way, how this path has to be sought in medicine, physiology and biology. In these lectures it will be our task to perceive how it must be sought if we are to form aright our general, human understanding of the world—which we so need in today's society.

Lecture 2

Yesterday I drew your attention to the fact that at the present period in human thought we compress the whole world within *abstract lines of space,* which stand perpendicular to one another and form the three dimensions of space, whereas life itself shows this three-dimensional world to be much more complicated and much more concrete. In order to gain an adequate conception of all that this means, we must grasp it in even greater definition.

If it is true that our thinking is associated with the vertical plane which cuts through our axis of symmetry, our willing with the vertical plane which stands perpendicularly to the thought-plane, while the plane of feeling rests at right angles to both, we must ask why we do not experience above and below, right and left, in front and behind, as three directions distinct in quality from each other and not interchangeable. How is it that we simply feel them as three space dimensions of equal value? We certainly speak of length, breadth and height, but if we form our three planes in this way, each at right angles to the other, we might place the line which was horizontal in the first instance in a vertical position, and the other two would then become horizontal. In short, we could make three different arrangements. This only shows that all the care and exactitude with which these three dimensions are built into the human body becomes quite abstract when used by man to describe and explain the whole universe with the sun and the stars.

It is important to ask how we manage to obtain abstract space dimensions from concrete ones. An animal could not do this! An animal would always feel its plane of symmetry as a concrete 'symmetry' plane, and it would not relate this symmetry plane to any abstract direction, but would at most, if it could think at all in the human sense, feel the rotation through different planes. The animal in fact *does* feel this rotation as a deviation of its symmetry plane from the normal. Herein lie important and essential problems of zoology, which will grow clear once man begins to study the true impulses at work here.

The reason that animals can find direction, as is shown most clearly of all in the case of the migration of birds, is because they do not feel the three directions of space in a nebulous way, but feel themselves as part of a quite definite direction of space, and feel each departure from this direction as an angle, as a deviation.

Now, if we wish to understand how all this applies to man, we must call to our assistance what we have already learned about the organization of the human body. We have heard that man is a threefold being, consisting firstly of the characteristic head organization, which does not of course include the head alone but chiefly functions there, and extends throughout the rest of the body. Then there is what I will designate 'circulation man'—all that belongs to lung and heart, and embodies rhythm in us. And lastly there is 'limb man', whose inward continuation constitutes metabolism or the transmutation of substance.

We now need to study this threefold man more closely. We will first think of him in terms of head, rhythm and limbs. Of these three, only the third with its continuation inwards is strongly connected with the forces—not the substances, but the *forces*—of our earthly planet.

This does not apply to 'head man', for what is he? (We are not now considering physical substance but the forces, the *formative forces* which condition him.) Head forces are the metamorphosis of the limb forces of the previous incarnation.

The forces that formed the limbs in the last incarnation, have, during the period between the last death and the latest birth—that birth which brought us into our present existence—been in a world which we have often described. There they were metamorphosed so that they could form our present head. Thus head forces and limb forces within us are complete polar opposites, and the central, mediating rhythmic forces in us create adjustment between the two, balancing or reconciling them by means of rhythm.

This antithesis between our head and limb forces must be examined further. We shall, perhaps, be able more easily to approach these matters if we examine the following example taken from another sphere.

Consider the plant—not, for the moment, a perennial plant, but an annual which develops from seed to root and stem, and during the year forms its fruit and seed. Such a plant grows from the seed that has been planted in the earth; out of the seed, in the course of the year, emerge the roots, then the leaves and the flowers, in which, during the fruit stage, the new seed develops. This is the cyclical development of the plant.

The plant proceeds from its seed in the earth, grows until it reaches the surface—where it receives the effects of light from the sun, and the effects of warmth. Under these influences it grows still further and completes its cycle by returning again to the stage of seed-formation. But now, when it returns to the seeding period in autumn we have the plant not below in the soil but above the earth; and here, all summer long, it has been dependent upon influences descending from beyond the earth. These influences helped to promote its growth to the point of new seed-formation; it has therefore grown to the point of a fresh seed-formation not under the influences of the earth, but while, one can say, drawn away from these by extra-terrestrial forces. It has become once more what it was before and yet something different. In what sense different? The completion of the new seed *terminates* the process of growth. Development ends here, and the cycle cannot be completed unless we take the seed from its own plane or region and return it once more to the earth. That is to say, if we follow that seed up into the sphere in which it is beyond the earthly element, we must then bring it down again, under the earth. Then once more it grows up towards heaven; and then again we must bring it down to earth once more. That is to say, further growth depends upon returning the seed to a lower level—we must return to earth what has been generated by celestial forces. Therefore it is not sufficient merely to consider the sequential cycle from seed to seed. We need to see that the plant in a sense outgrows itself, and when it has outgrown itself to a certain stage, we must bring it back again to its original starting point, where it is once more received by the same forces, and the cycle begins anew.

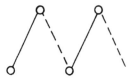

We can now draw the process in a diagram. If this is the earth level here, then the cycle of evolution for the plant must be drawn thus. But the plant must again return to earth, and so if we draw several annual processes, we must advance a little further each time. There you have the difference of level. We must continually return the plant to a lower level.

I have given you this as an illustration, and before we pass on, something else must be considered in connection with it. Notice the way in which the bean plant arises out of the seed, and you will understand what I mean. You will realize it still better if you observe a plant with a twining stem, one that is naturally inclined not to grow up in a straight line if certain forces are able to act freely. The bindweed is an instance of such a plant.

Now let us pass on to consider this picture in connection with man. If instead of thinking of the yearly cycle of the plant we turn our attention to that cycle which leads man from one earthly life, through the spiritual world, to the next earthly life, we have there something quite remarkably similar. Think of your limb organism in the previous incarnation, and your head in this incarnation. The head is formed through a metamorphosis, and it is only *visible* change that is interrupted by all that takes place between death and a new birth. The head is formed in the same way as the new seed in the plant is formed out of the old. But the whole of the intermediate life of the plant lies between. Thus from the point of view of the organization of his form, it is as if in man the root existed in the previous incarnation, and out of this root has grown the head of the present incarnation. The head, therefore, represents something analogous to the seed. But in man all this takes place, one may say, at a higher level—in a higher region—and is, besides, more complex.

And now in order to complete this picture, think of the whole metamorphosis of the plant. If you observe bindweed, you will see from the spiral or screw-like form of the stem that external forces are not such as to cause it merely to grow in a straight line, but induce it to grow in a spiral form. The plant has a tendency to spiral formation. Only when the *new seed* is developed does the seed resist this tendency, for then everything is entirely concentrated in this small grain. The seed withdraws from the influence of the universe. In the case of man, limb forces are most subject to the earth's influence. (In our rhythmic region things are different and we will speak about this later.) But the head is something which withdraws itself from earthly forces and takes no part in them, just as the seed takes no part in the external influences. Only because the head withdraws from earthly forces are we able to think in abstract thoughts. Were it impossible for our head to separate itself entirely from earthly influences, we could not think in the abstract.

This fact is actually expressed in man's very form. Think for a moment that your head actually embodies transformed limb forces. The latter however are active in walking upon the earth's surface, not so the head. The head may be compared with a man who is comfortably seated in a motor car or in a train; he does not move and yet goes forward. The head is in this position in respect to the rest of the organism; the latter advances, moves forward, while the head rests as though in a vehicle, not taking part in any of the movements, but withdrawing itself in a very evident way from earthly forces. The head is like the man who lets himself be transported by other people.

Such is man's head organization. It withdraws from the earth's influences, and we can therefore say: The head of man shows itself—at least in this comparison—similar to the seed that withdraws from the external, formative influences at work on the plant. But with man it is not the same as with the plant. The latter grows from the earth upwards—towards the celestial influences. Man grows downwards. When he arrives at conception or birth, he is in the first place a head structure; external embryology affords absolute proof of this. He brings with him his head as a transformed product of the last incarnation. During this earthly life—through the forces of it— what most develops are our limbs. These grow from the head.

They are less evolved than the head and entirely under the influence of earthly forces. The head on the other hand is entirely withdrawn from earthly forces. Thus, in observing plants, we can trace in their spiral formation the forces that give the plant its twisting, winding form, derived from celestial bodies. But when we consider man, and see how he grows down towards the earth, we must ask what has given him the capacity to grow in opposition to the laws governing the ascending growth of the plant. For man grows downwards and gradually becomes subject to earthly influence. What is the explanation for all this? This is a most important, indeed an essential question, concerning not only morphology, the study of the human form, but man's whole being. You see, if we were obliged to live our inner life without a head, it would be entirely different; we would be incapable of any abstract ideas! Above all, we would not be able to conceive of three-dimensional space as abstract, but would strictly differentiate between front and back, right and left, above and below. All these directions would be for us quite distinct in character. This is, in fact, what our *organism* does. As soon as you advance, through the methods of spiritual science, to an imaginative conception of the universe, a comfortably abstract three-dimensionality ceases. Then you inevitably become aware of real distinctions, for you have performed something quite remarkable—you have eliminated the ordinary organism of the head and have returned to man's *etheric organism.*

Now the etheric organization is essentially different from the physical organization of the head. It is only through the fully developed head, achieved in this incarnation as a result of the previous one, that abstractions become possible. All abstract thinking, all thinking on the plane of pure thought, is bound to this head organism, which we attain only by leaving the spiritual world and coming into this physical world, in order to make independent of our earthly organization something that was formerly dependent on it.

This will show you that man, like the plant, is embedded in earthly influences; but with this difference—that man makes himself independent of them through his head organism. If the rest of our organism were to think without the head—as indeed it can—man would at once feel himself one with the whole organism of the universe.

If it were possible to invent a very comfortable 'sleeping car'—it is at the present time perhaps unlikely—but a car from which you did not look out and from which all noise and rattle were eliminated, you might fall into the illusion that you were in a still and silent room, for you would perceive nothing of its movement. But upon looking out of the window, you would see that it is moving forward, although you are sitting quietly in the car. Similarly, as soon as you also release yourself from the illusion which your head organism produces in you during the process of making itself independent of the earth-organization, you will observe that you are taking part in the earth's motion. That is to say, it is possible, through the transition from what, in my book *How To Know Higher Worlds*, I have called the present-day mode of forming ideas, to what I have called Imagination—it is possible to *feel the movements of the earth*, because you are then 'looking out of the window', looking into the spiritual world. In just the same way as you look through the window of a train and notice the landscape outside continually changing, so do you when looking out of the physical sense-world into the spiritual perceive in the alterations in the latter, as you pass by, that you and the earth are not at rest, but moving forward together. Hence we cannot arrive at a true spatial image of the cosmos in astronomy if we insist upon constructing it just with that part of our organism which has made itself independent!

Consider for a moment what we as civilized humanity have done since the beginning of this fifth post-Atlantean epoch. We have thought about the universe with our head. And it is the head—that part of us which has made itself quite inde-

pendent of the earth—that has condensed planetary movements into the abstract three dimensions. We have the
Copernican conception of the universe, designed for us by *the
least appropriate* means, the head, the essential characteristic
of which is its emancipation from involvement in cosmic
movements. It would be somewhat as though you wished to
obtain an idea, shall we say, of the movement of a railway train
in which you are travelling from a picture of it you draw with
your hand without reference to the movement of the train, but
solely according to your own ideas. You draw something; you
make yourself independent. But you cannot consider such a
drawing as depicting the actual movement of the railway train;
it has nothing whatever to do with it! And just as little to do
with the world-process has a picture of it that we have
designed according to external spatial astronomy, using for
the purpose the means that are the most inadequate for its
conception.

Now just observe to what conclusion a conception of things
invested with reality leads us. We are then compelled to admit
that our spatial, astronomical picture of the world has been
built up with the most inadequate means. No wonder it
contradicts the results that are obtained when the right means
are used! Of course, for certain purposes this view of things is
well adapted, because since the middle of the fifteenth century, when the fifth post-Atlantean period began, we have had
gradually to learn to form thoughts independently of the
universe. We shall hear in the next lecture how that came
about. But we have thereby lost the capacity to really know
anything of the movements we undergo together with the
earth, and which then surface when we train ourselves to feel
concretely the otherwise abstract dimensions of space. We
shall continually deepen our understanding of these things;
for we cannot arrive at a complete picture in any other way
than by building up our ideas in cycles, as it were.

After yesterday's lecture Dr Stein has taken the trouble to

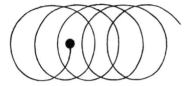

construct a model showing the movements which result when we observe *man together with the earth*, or in other words the movement of the earth taken in its absolute sense. If, instead of following the motion of plant forces in spirals, I follow the movements described by man with the earth, I again find a spiral, but one which is progressive. This spiral gives us an illustration of the real movement of the earth, and at the same time a picture of that of the sun. Suppose for a moment that the earth is here and the sun there. An observer sees the sun in this direction (diagram). The earth progresses, but exactly in a line behind the sun. When the earth is here, the observer now sees the sun in another direction. The sun advances still further, the earth following, and once again the observer sees the sun in the other direction. That is to say, he sees the sun at one time on the right, and another time on the left, owing to the way in which the earth follows the sun.

This has been interpreted as demonstrating that the sun stands still and the earth revolves round it. In reality, it is not so: the earth moves along behind the sun. The observer sees the sun to the right when the latter has arrived at one point of the spiral path, while the earth is here. Next he sees the sun to the left, then again right, then left, and so on. All this gives the observer, who judges by outward appearances and loses sight of his own movement, the impression that the earth revolves round the sun.

From this you will realize how great a possibility of deception arises when one judges by exterior appearances; for here indeed a relativity of motion exists. We can really affirm that those who now calculate the apparent motion of the sun do not perceive their own motion, and omit to take into consideration the relation between the sun and the earth.

I should like you to try to form a true idea of what I have said about course or motion in a spiralling line, because one must visualize, in a model such as this, the fact of the earth following in the wake of the sun; and then we shall be able to go on to what I should like us to achieve tomorrow, namely, a true understanding of the facts before us. Today I have intentionally given suggestions only, and purposely left many questions open, but they will be answered tomorrow or in one of the subsequent lectures. I wanted to show you in a quite simple way the experiences of one who looks out through the windows of the physical world, and observes the spiritual world outside as it rushes by. In this way he can form an idea of the real motion of the earth and also of the sun.

But I will show you first how to gain a conception of the true relation of the earth to the sun—that the earth actually *follows* the sun in its path—by searching for the one thing that will show us this relationship, namely, certain processes in the human organism connected with the embodiment of the sun in man—the human heart. For it is by taking our start from the knowledge of *man* that we must seek to attain a knowledge of the *universe*.

Lecture 3

In these studies I wanted to draw your attention to certain things which can lead us back to a more concrete study of the universe than is contained in the Copernican world view. We must not forget that Copernican cosmogony arose during the epoch after the middle of the fifteenth century when there was an increasing tendency towards abstract conceptions of the universe. It came indeed at a time when the tendency to make everything abstract was at its height. We must also remember that it is essential now that we should get free of this tendency and bring to our thought about the universe concepts that contain something more than merely abstract ideas. It is not a matter simply of constructing a world view similar to that of Copernicus, on slightly different lines. This was brought home to me in the questions arising out of the last lecture. For these questions turned on the possibility of being able, yet again, to draw lines that would give us a quite external, abstract picture of the world. That of course is not what is needed. What we have to do is to grasp in its spiritual nature all that is *not* man, in order to build a bridge from the spiritual in man to the spiritual outside him. You must understand that here, at this particular time at all events, it cannot be our task to discuss a mathematical astronomy. That would necessitate beginning over again from elementary rudiments, for the fundamental concepts employed today have their source in the whole materialistic mode of thinking that has arisen since the middle of the fifteenth century. If we wanted to develop and complete the world view we have sketched, it would be necessary to begin with the most elementary principles and elaborate them anew. The fate that befell Copernicanism came about, as we shall see, because of the strong tendency to abstraction, which may so easily lead to intellectual excesses. True Copernicanism is not really the same as that which it has become in the hands of the followers of Copernicus. Certain theories have been selected from Copernicanism which were quite in keeping with the ways of thought of the last few centuries, and from them the world view now taught in all schools has arisen.

It is not my wish to offer any similar type of cosmogony— where, instead of the well-known ellipse in which the sun is placed as one of the foci, and in which the earth moves with an inclined axis, we simply put a screw-shaped line! What I want to do instead is to describe man's relationship with the universe; and it is in this direction that we will now pursue the matter further.

I have tried to show you how, the moment one begins to pass to a more intensive, inner experience of the three directions of space in one's own body, one realizes how these directions differ in nature and kind from one another; it is only the faculty of mental abstraction in the head which makes these three dimensions abstract and does not distinguish between above and below, left and right, before and behind, but simply takes them as three directions. And we would immediately commit a similar error, if we set out to build any other spatial construct in a purely abstract way. The point at issue can be made clearer if for a moment we turn to something else.

Let us consider *colours* once more. Suppose we have a blue surface and, let us say, a yellow one. The conception of the world which, in its abstract thinking, gave rise to Copernican cosmogony has also led us to say: 'I see before me blue, I see before me yellow. That is due to the fact that some object has made an impression on me. This impression appears to me as yellow, as blue.' The point is that we should not begin to theorize in this way at all, saying: 'Before me is yellow, before me is blue, and they make a certain impression upon me.' That is really just as if you were to treat the word PICTURE in the following way. Suppose you were to set about making deep researches into the word and think: ' "P", something must underlie this; behind "P" I must seek the vibrations which cause it. Then again, behind the "I" there must be vibrations, and underlying the "C" more vibrations, and so on.' There is no sense in this. We find sense only when we unite the seven letters, connecting one with another in their own plane, and read the whole word 'Picture'; when we do not speculate as to what underlies each letter, but read the word itself. Here too, likewise, we should say that the first surface (blue) makes me penetrate, as it were, behind it, makes me plunge into it, while the other surface (yellow) makes me turn away from it. It is to these *feelings* into which impressions transform that we must pay attention; then we come to something concrete. If we thus seek in the world outside what we experience inwardly, we come indeed to the feeling that we are not really *within ourself* at all, but that our real ego is *in the universe*, poured out into the universe. Instead of searching behind the external universe for 'vibrations', the atomists should seek for their own ego behind the phenomena and then try to find out how their own ego is placed into the outer world, is, as it were, poured out into it. Just as with colour we should try to ascertain whether we feel we must plunge into it or whether we feel ourselves repulsed by it, so, as regards the structure of our organism, we should feel how the three directions, above and below, forwards and backwards, right and left, differ concretely from one another; we should feel how differently is our inward experience of them when we project ourselves into the world. When we are aware of ourselves as human beings upon the earth, surrounded by the planets and fixed stars, we begin to feel ourselves as part of all these; it is not a matter merely of drawing three dimensions at right angles, but of thinking concretely about the cosmos and penetrating into the concrete reality of the dimensions of space.

Now there is a series of constellations that is immediately evident to those who study the outer universe at night-time, and has indeed always been seen as long as people have studied the stars. It is what we call the *zodiac*. It is immaterial whether we believe in the Ptolemaic or the Copernican system; if we follow the apparent course of the sun it always seems to pass through the zodiac in its yearly round. Now if we imagine ourselves placed into the universe in a living way, we find that the zodiac is of very great significance. We cannot conceive of any other plane in celestial space as being of like value with the zodiac, any more than we could conceive the plane which divides us in two and creates our symmetry as being placed at random just anywhere. We then perceive the zodiac as something through which a plane may be described (*drawing*). Let us suppose this plane to be the plane of the blackboard, so that we have here the plane of the zodiac; the plane of the zodiac is plain to see here as the plane of the blackboard.* We shall then have one plane before us in cosmic space, precisely as we imagined the three planes embodied in man. That is certainly a plane of which we can say that it is fixed there for us. We see the sun run its course through the zodiac, and we relate all the phenomena of the heavens to this plane. And we have here an analogy from the celestial world outside man for what we must perceive and experience as planes in man himself. Now when we draw the symmetry plane in man, and have on one side of the symmetry-axis the liver organized in one way, and on the other side the stomach organized in a different way, we cannot think of such a fact without feeling at the same time some

---

* A play on words here in the original German: '. . . so daß seine Ebene eben die Ebene der Tafel sei.'

inner concrete relation. We cannot imagine mere lines of space lying there, but what is in the space must manifest definite forces of activity—it will not be a matter of indifference whether something is on the right or on the left. In the same way we must imagine that in the organization of the universe it is a matter of consequence whether a thing is above or below the zodiac. We shall begin to think of cosmic space—as we see it there, sown with stars—we shall begin to think of it as having *form*.

Now just as we can think of this plane on the blackboard, so we can also think of another at right angles to it. Let us think of a plane extending from the constellation Leo to that of Aquarius on the other side. Then we can go further and imagine a third plane at right angles again to this one, running from Taurus to Scorpio. We have now three planes at right angles to one another in cosmic space.

These three planes are analogous to the three we have imagined in man. If we think of the plane we have denoted as that of will—the plane, that is, which separates our front from our back—we have the plane of the zodiac itself.

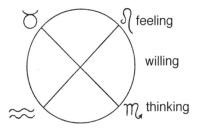

If we think of the plane running from Taurus to Scorpio, we have the plane of thinking; that is, our thought plane would be ascribed to this plane. And the third plane would be that of feeling. Thus we have divided cosmic space by means of three planes, just as we divided man in our first lecture.

What is important initially is *not* simply to replace the Copernican cosmic system with some other, but to enter into this concrete picture, to imagine cosmic space itself so organized that one can distinguish in it three planes at right angles to one another, just as can be done in the case of man.

The next question to arise for us must be: Is every single aspect of man really to be conceived as forming an integral part of what appears to us in outer cosmogony? We emphasized in the last lecture that the earth, the sun and other planets progress in a spiral. Such a statement is, of course, merely diagrammatic, for the spiral line itself is curved. That however does not concern us here; what is important for us at the moment is that the earth, as we have seen, follows the sun in such a spiral, so we must ask whether man too is so interwoven in this movement that he is absolutely compelled to take part in it in all circumstances; for if that be so, if it is absolutely inevitable that he follows this movement, then there is no place at all for free will or for moral activity on his part. Let us not forget that we began our study with this very question: how to build a bridge leading from pure natural *necessity* to *morality*, to what is motivated by the impulse towards freedom.

Here we can go no further if we rely only on the Copernican system, for what does this offer us? We picture the earth upon which we stand—whether the earth or the sun goes rushing along has no bearing here. If man is connected with all this in absolute natural causality, it is impossible for him to develop free will. We must therefore ask whether the entire being of man lies bound within this natural causality, or whether we ever get beyond it. We must not however put the question in a mood of thought similar to nineteenth-century materialists, who pointed out that so many people have died on earth that it would not be possible to find space to fit all their souls. These materialists were wondering how much space each soul might need. But what point does it really have to ask such a question?

We must above all clearly understand that the full sense and meaning of phenomena in the universe—and movement is also a phenomenon—only becomes clear to us when we grasp it in specific cases. We distinguish in some way what takes place in the four, or eight, realms—what is above and below the plane of the zodiac (will), and what is right and left of the plane of feeling; or what lies on this or on the other side of the plane of thinking. We feel that something is connected with this differentiation, a reality connected with the cosmos, namely, something that manifests in recapitulation, as we have it for instance in what we designate as the 'course of the year'. And we must now ask in a concrete way: How can we find a connection between man and the yearly course of the seasons? Well, first of all we find that in descending from the spiritual world into the physical, we pass through conception. We remain for about nine months in the embryonic condition—that is to say, *three months fewer* than the year's course. We might be inclined to call this, therefore, something very much at odds with the cycle of the seasons. Man seems to show, even at the very genesis of his physical earthly existence, that his development pays no attention to the course of cyclical rhythms in nature. This is however not the case. If we know how to observe the child during the first three months of his earthly life, we find that these first three months—which, together with the nine months of pregnancy, make the year complete—manifest in a very true sense a continuation of his embryonic life; what takes place in the brain, as well as other things happening with the little child, can from a certain aspect be considered as still belonging to his embryonic life. Thus we can say that in a certain respect the first year of human development corresponds, after all, with the year's course.

Then comes another year—or about a year. If we observe the child after the first year, we see that the second year is approximately the time of the growth of the milk teeth. We observe the child during the second year after its conception, and we find that this year corresponds on average with the growth of the first teeth. Now let us ask, does this continue? No, it does not. The first 'teething' year seems to represent an inner cycle of seasons within the child. And so it does, just as the first year of life, including nine months in the womb, is at the same time an inner cycle of the year. In the formation of the milk teeth, the universe obviously works in the child. But then something different happens.

In a space of time seven times as long, the force which pushes out the second teeth is at work in the child. Here something occurs which we cannot connect with the world's course but with something that is withdrawn out of it, and works out of our inner being.

Here, then, we have a concrete instance. We have, first of all, in respect to one series of facts, the world organism projected into man in the formation of his milk teeth. And then, when we look at the permanent teeth, we find that these are man's own production. An inner *human* cosmic system places them into the outer cosmic system. Here we have the first herald of man's potential freedom, in the fact that he engages in something which clearly shows his independence from the universe. This process retains the sequence of the universe within it but man slows it down within him, giving the same process a different velocity, seven times as slow, thus taking seven times as long. Here we have a contrast between what takes place within us and the outer being of the universe.

Another independence from the outer universe is very clearly demonstrated in the alternation between sleeping and waking. The alternation between day and night takes place, of course, at different times for different places on the earth. What does this alternation between waking and sleeping mean for us?

Roughly speaking, it means that sometimes our ego and astral body are united with our etheric and physical bodies, and at other times our ego and astral body are separated from the etheric and physical bodies.

Now someone in the present cycle of civilization, especially one who calls himself a civilized person, is no longer entirely dependent in this respect on the natural cycle. The cycle of waking and sleeping, in its measure of time, seems to resemble the cycle of nature; but nowadays there are people— I have known such!—who turn night into day and day into night. In short, we can wrest ourselves free from connection with the world's course. The sequence in us of the sleeping and waking states shows however that we still have within us an echo of this regularity. The same is true of many phenomena in the human being. When we observe our alternation between waking and sleeping, and nature's alternation between day and night, and how we are still bound to the alternation of waking and sleeping though not to that of day and night, we must say: Man's inner states were once bound to the outer course of the universe, but he has broken away from this. Civilized human beings nowadays have almost entirely broken away from the course of outer nature. Only when we perceive, when we discover with our intellect, that it is better for us to sleep at night rather than by day, do we consciously return to outer laws. It is not the case, however, that night takes possession of us in such a way that we absolutely have to sleep. No civilized person really feels: 'Night makes me sleep, day wakes me up.' At most, if night falls and a lecture is still going on here, the two facts taken together may perhaps affect some in such a way that they experience an absolute call of nature to fall asleep. These however are not necessarily things we need to include in our picture of the world!

Thus the point to observe is that we have wrested ourselves away from the course of nature, but that the rhythms of our activity nevertheless still show a reflection of it. Let us see how transitions from one to the other condition manifest themselves. We may say that in our waking and sleeping we still distinctly show a reflection of the course of nature, but that we

have wrested ourselves free from it. In the appearance of the
second teeth, we no longer reveal a chronology at one with
nature such as is still expressed in the growth of the first teeth.
When we receive our second teeth, a new course of nature
arises in us; for this is not in our control like sleeping and
waking. Our free choice does not enter here. Here something
appears that belongs to nature yet does not follow the larger
course of nature, something which is particular to man. And
yet it is not within his free choice, it is implanted as a second
natural organization within the first.

In all these things, I am speaking of quite simple everyday
matters, but it is a question of noticing them in the right way.
We must now examine the fact that there is a certain natural
'event', which is interwoven with the growth of the first teeth.
Let us draw it in diagram. Within this natural event or process, as a part of the process, the formation of our first teeth
proceeds. Then we have another natural occurrence, one
intrinsically human, not at all embedded in the general course
of world phenomena—the growth of the second teeth (red).
To draw this, we must present it as a different stream. Yet the
difference is not yet clear in the drawing, they both look alike.
The fact is, we must represent it in a quite different way if we
want to depict the connection between the receiving of the
first and second teeth: we must draw what gives rise to the first
teeth as occurring seven times deeper for the second teeth. If
we draw them side by side, parallel, we have no picture of the

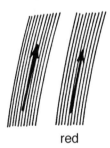

red

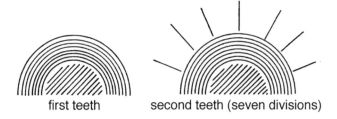

first teeth   second teeth (seven divisions)

relation of the first teeth to the second; we only get a picture of this by drawing the force giving rise to the first teeth as encircled by another force, upon which the growth of the second teeth depends. Here, the difference in speed of the process makes it necessary for the movement to *curve*. You can imagine it in terms of a star somewhere in space with another circling round it, whose orbit exerts an influence at seven different points, say, as it passes round. The simple fact of the revolution gives rise to something qualitative—a creative activity.

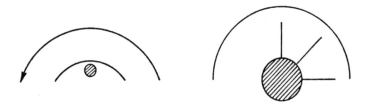

Looking at the growth of the first teeth and of the second we must therefore say that this has something to do with certain world forces, one of which circles round the other. I put this example before you, because it can show what it means to speak of real, actual movements in space, and how empty is the kind of talk which says: Jupiter—or, it may be Saturn—is so and so many miles distant from the sun and encircles it in such and such a line. That tells one nothing at all, it is an empty phrase. We can only know anything about facts like these when we unite some content with them, such as: the

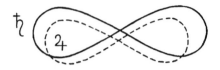

orbit of Jupiter is like this, the orbit of Saturn like that, and the revolution of the one serves the revolution of the other.

I have here merely pointed out the necessity inherent in certain specific processes. Some of you may say that they are difficult to understand. Or perhaps you will not say so, but will consider that there is no need to discuss them! Not until people learn to discuss and study such things will they be able to progress to a definite and clear view of the universe. And then they will give up what is presented so superficially in Copernicanism—the conception of the celestial movements solely in lines. Instead of this an impulse should enter humanity which says: It is necessary to be clear first about our own most elementary experiences before turning our attention to the outer mysteries of the universe.

We only learn the significance of certain interconnections which we read from the stars, when we understand the corresponding processes in our organism; for what lies within our skin is no other than a reflection of the organism of the outer world. Thus if we draw a diagram of the human being, we have here the blood circulation, merely in diagrammatic form, and we can trace its path. It is all within us. If we now go out into the universe and look for the sun, it is the sun which corresponds to the heart within us. What passes from the heart through the body, or actually from the body to the heart, does in truth approximately resemble the movements connected with the course of the sun. Instead of drawing abstract lines, we should look into the human being. Within our own skin we can then find what is outside in celestial space, and can see how we are embedded in the cosmic order. At the same time we can also discover that we are independent of the cosmic system, and that we gradually gain this independence little by little, as I have shown. We will speak further about this in the next lecture; for the present we must realize that we are dealing with it here merely in a diagrammatic way.

Look at the principal course of the blood-vessels in the human organism. Seen from above it is like a looped line. Instead of drawing it, we should follow the hieroglyphs inscribed in our own selves; for then we would learn to understand the nature of the qualities in the greater universe. This we can only do when we are able to recognize and have living experience of the fact I have spoken about in public lectures: that the heart does not work like a pump driving the blood through the body, but that the heart is moved by the circulation, which is itself a living thing, and the circulation is in its turn determined by the organs. The heart, as can be seen in embryology, is really nothing more than a *result* of blood circulation. If we can understand what the heart is in the human body, we shall learn to understand also that the sun is not, as Newton calls it, the general cable-pulley sending its ropes (the force of gravitation) towards the planets. Mercury, Venus, Earth, Mars and so forth, drawing them by these unseen forces of attraction, or spraying out light to them, and the like; but that just as the movement of the heart is the product of the life-force of the circulation, so the sun is no other than the product of the whole planetary system. The sun is the *result*, not the point of departure. The living co-operation of the solar system produces in the centre a hollow, which reflects as a mirror. That is the sun! I have often said that physicists would be greatly astonished if they could travel to the sun. They would find nothing of what they now imagine, but simply a hollow space—in fact a hollow space of suction which annihilates everything within it. A space indeed that is more than hollow. A hollow space merely receives what is put into it; but the sun is a hollow space of such a nature that anything brought to it is immediately absorbed and disappears. There in the sun is not only nothing, but less than nothing. What shines to us in the light is the reflection of what first enters from cosmic space—just as the movement of the heart is, as it were, what accumulates and condenses there out of the living activity of hunger and thirst etc. in the interaction of organs and movement of blood.

If we understand the processes within our organism, they can also enable us to understand the processes at work in outer cosmic space. The abstract dimensions of space are only a prop to help us follow these things more easily. But if we wish to follow them up in a truthful way, we must try to experience ourselves inwardly, and then turn outwards with inner understanding. They understand the sun who understand the human heart; and so it is with the rest of what occurs within us.

Thus it is a matter of supreme importance to take the saying 'Know Thyself' seriously, and from that to pass on to comprehension of the universe. Through self-knowledge which embraces our whole being, we shall understand the universe outside us.

You see we cannot get on so quickly with constructing a cosmogony! In order to make a few of the features of this cosmogony clear, we can of course draw a spiral; but this does not yet show the actual state of things. For to describe a few more features, we must make the spiral itself move spirally; we must make the line of movement itself curve. And even then we have not come far, for in order to describe certain facts such as the difference between the growth of the first year's teeth and the growth of the seven years' teeth must describe an inner displacement within the line itself.

So you see that the construction of a universe is not a thing that can be done very quickly. The wish to construct a cosmogony with a few lines must be relinquished, and we must learn to regard our present conception of the world as an absolute delusion.

This is intended as a preparatory study for what I mean to say in the next lecture. It had to be rather more difficult; but once these initial difficulties are overcome, we shall have constructed the preliminary conditions for uniting the three important domains of life—*nature, morality* and *religion*—by means of two corresponding bridges.

Lecture 4

The universe cannot actually be observed or imagined at all without continual reference to man, without continually trying to find in the wider universe what exists in one way or another in ourselves. In these lectures we will try to obtain at least one aspect of a kind of overall structural picture of the world, which can then lead us to answer the question: What is the relation between morality and natural law in the human being?

When we study the human being (I am here only repeating things that have already been spoken and written about from various perspectives) we find him first of all organized into what we may call upper and lower realms; and then we have what forms the connection between the two—the rhythmic region, equalizing or balancing the other two parts.

We have to observe first of all that there is a radical difference between the laws governing the upper and lower realms. We can realize this difference when we consider the fact that the upper realm, which is regulated by the head, is in its origin the outcome of entirely different laws than those of the sense world.

That part of us which in our last incarnation was a result of forces of the sense world, namely, the limb realm, has become what it now is, the head realm, through a metamorphosis *which takes place between death and a new birth*—not in relation, of course, to the outer form, but in regard to its formative forces. The forces at present active in our limbs become entirely transformed. Their supersensible constitution is transmuted between death and a new birth, and appears in our new earth life incorporated out of the universe into our head constitution. To this is attached, as it were, the rest of man—formed out of the sense world. Embryology could clearly demonstrate this if we would only relate embryological phenomena to one another in a sensible way. And thus we have in our head-organization a lawfulness not belonging to this world at all, save only at its origin—that is, in so far as it was present in a previous incarnation. But all that which has caused the transformation of limb forces to head forces is active in an entirely different world—the world in which we live between death and a new birth. Here, then, another world penetrates the world of the senses. Another world is manifested in our head organism. In a certain sense the external world is brought into correspondence with this other world, in that the head projects the principal sense-organs outwards. The world that extends through space and runs its course in time, is perceived by our senses; it penetrates into us through our senses, and so it too, after all, belongs in a certain sense to the head organism. In relation to our limb realm, on the other hand, we are in a state of sleep. I have often spoken of this sleep-state of man in relation to his will nature, in relation to all that lives in the limb realm. We do not know *how* we move our limbs, *how* the will causes the movement; we only examine the movement afterwards as an outer phenomenon through our senses. We are asleep in our limb-organization, in the same sense as we are asleep in the universe between going to sleep and awaking.

So here we have before us an entirely different world. We can say that we have, firstly, a world which outwardly manifests all that speaks to our senses, all that we perceive through eyes, ears, etc. To this world we belong through that portion of ourselves which we have called the *head* realm. But our connection with the other world that lies *behind* this one arises through our limbs, a realm in which we are unconscious; we sleep into this world, whether we do so in the domain of our will, or whether we sleep into the universe between going to sleep and waking.

These two worlds are actually so constituted that the one is turned towards us, and the other away from us, as it were; the latter lies behind the world of sense although we have our origin in it. Man felt in olden times—and the East still feels it—that a reconciliation between the two is possible. As you know, we in the West search for the reconciliation in a different way; but in the Orient, even today, people still attempt to find it in a relatively conscious way, although their approach is nowadays outdated for present-day humanity. When we eat, the process takes place in the sphere of sleep (unconsciously). We are not aware of what is really happening when we eat an egg or a cabbage; it takes place in the unconscious like sleep. The cabbage and the egg manifest their exterior to our sense-perception. But the eating really belongs to a completely different world. Mediation between these two worlds, however, is to be found in our breathing.

Although the latter is to a certain extent unconscious, it is not as unconscious as our digestion. In spite of the fact that our breathing is not as conscious as our hearing and seeing, it is more conscious than a process such as digestion; and while in the East today the attempt to make the digestive process a conscious one has, as a rule, ceased (this used to be done in olden times), the breathing process is still made conscious in a particular way. (Snakes raise the process of digestion into consciousness, but the consciousness of the snake is of course not human consciousness. Ruminants do this too.) There is a certain training of the breathing, where inhaling and exhaling are regulated in such a way that the process is transformed into a sense-perception. Thus we find respiration placed, as it were, between conscious sense-perception and the complete unconsciousness of assimilation and transmutation of physical matter. Man in fact dwells in three worlds; the one of which he is consciously aware, the other of which he remains entirely unconscious, and the third (breathing) acting as a connecting link or mediator between the two.

Now it is a fact that the process of breathing is also a kind of assimilation; at all events, it is a material process, though taking place in a more rarefied manner. It is an intermediate state between actual transmutation of matter (assimilation) and the process of sense-perception, the completely conscious experience of the external world.

In the state in which we find ourselves between falling asleep and awaking, we experience in the environment which then surrounds us events which only enter into our normal consciousness as dreams. Here man steps across into the other, different world I have spoken of, and the dreams reveal through their very nature how we step across. Consider for a moment how nearly related are dreams to the process of respiration—the rhythm of breathing—how often you can trace the after-effect of this rhythm when you dream. Man steps across the border, as it were, of the world of consciousness, when he dips ever so slightly into this other world in which he is when he sleeps or when he dreams. There lies also the world of 'imaginations'. In imaginative perception this becomes a fully conscious world for us; we have conscious perception there which we merely sip, as it were, in our dreams.

We shall now have to consider a correspondence that is found to exist, an absolute correspondence, in respect of number. I have already often drawn your attention to this correspondence between man and the world in which he evolves. I have pointed to the fact that our rhythm of breathing—18 breaths per minute—manifests something that is in remarkable accord with other processes of the universe. We take 18 breaths per minute, which over a whole day comes to 25,920 respirations. And we arrive at the same number when we calculate how many days are contained in a normal life term of 72 years. That also gives about 25,920 days; so that something may be said to exhale our astral body and ego on falling asleep, and inhale them again upon waking—always in conformity with the same number rhythm.

And again, when we consider how the sun moves—whether apparently or really, does not matter—advancing a little each year in what we call the precession of the equinoxes, when we consider the number of years it takes the sun to make this journey round the whole zodiac, once more we get 25,920 years—the Platonic year.

The fact is that within the boundaries set by birth and death, this human life of ours is indeed fashioned, down to its most infinitesimal processes—as we have seen in breathing—in accordance with the laws of the universe. But in the correspondence we have observed up to now between the macrocosm and man the microcosm, we have made our observations in a realm where the correspondence is obvious and evident. There are, however, other very important correspondences. For example, consider the following. I want to lead you through number to something else. Take the 18 respirations per minute, making 1,080 per hour and in 24 hours 25,920 respirations; that is, we must multiply $18 \times 60 \times 24$ in order to arrive at 25,920.

Taking this as the cycle of the precession of the equinoxes, and dividing it by 60 and again by 24, we would naturally get *18 years*. And what do these 18 years really mean? Consider—these 25,920 respirations correspond to a human day of 24 hours; in other words, this 24-hour day is the day of the microcosm. Eighteen respirations may serve as the unit of rhythm.

And now take the complete circle described by the precession of the equinoxes, and call it, not a Platonic year, but a great Day of the heavens, a macrocosmic day. How long would one respiration on this scale have to occupy to correspond with human respiration? Its duration would have to be 18 years—a respiration made by the being of the macrocosm.

Taking the statements of modern astronomy—we need not interpret them here, we shall speak of their meaning later—let us now examine what modern astronomers call *nutation of the earth's axis*.

You are aware that the earth's axis lies obliquely upon the ecliptic, and that astronomers speak of an oscillation of the earth's axis around this point and they call this 'nutation'. The axis completes one revolution around this point in just about 18 years (it is really 18 years, 7 months, but we need not consider the fraction, although it is quite possible to calculate this too with exactitude). But with these 18 years something else is intimately connected. For it is not merely on the fact of 'nutation'—this 'trembling', this rotation of the earth's axis in a double cone around the earth's centre, and the period of 18 years for its completion—it is not only on this fact that we have to fix our minds, but we find that simultaneously with it another process takes place. The moon appears each year in a different position because, like the sun, it ascends and descends from the ecliptic, proceeding in a kind of oscillating motion again and again towards the equator ecliptic. And every 18 years it appears once more in the same position it occupied 18 years before. You see there is a connection between this nutation and the path of the moon. Nutation is in truth nothing other than the moon's path. It is the projection of the motion of the moon, so that we can actually observe the 'breathing' of the macrocosm. We only need notice the path of the moon in 18 years or, in other words, the nutation of the earth's axis. The earth dances, and in such a manner as to describe a cone, a double cone, in 18 years, and this dancing is a reflection of the macrocosmic breathing. This takes place just as many times in the macrocosmic year as the 18 human respirations during the microcosmic day of 24 hours.

So we really have one macrocosmic respiration per minute in this nutation movement. In other words, we observe this breathing of the macrocosm through nutation or the movement of the moon, and we have before us what corresponds to respiration in man. And now, what does all this mean? The meaning of it is that as we pass from waking to sleep, or only from the wholly conscious to the dream state, we enter another world, and in contrast to the ordinary laws of day, years, etc., and also the Platonic year, we find in this insertion of a *moon* rhythm, something that has the same relationship in the macrocosm that breathing, the semiconscious process of respiration, has to our full consciousness. We have therefore not only to consider a world which is spread out before us, but another world which projects into, and permeates our own.

Just as we have before us a second part of the human organism, when observing the breathing process, namely the rhythmic realm, as opposed to the perceptive or head realm, so we have in what appears as the yearly moon motion, or rather the 18-year motion of the moon, the identity between one year and one human respiration; we have this second world interpenetrating our own.

There can therefore be no question of inhabiting only one world. We have the world that we can observe as the world of the senses; but then we have a world, underpinned by other laws, which stands in exactly the same relationship to the world of the senses, as our breathing does to our consciousness; and this other world is revealed to us as soon as we interpret in the right way this moon movement, this nutation of the earth's axis.

These considerations should enable you to realize the impossibilty of investigating in a one-sided way the laws manifesting in the world. The modern materialistic thinker is in quest of a single system of natural laws. In this he deludes himself; what he should say is, rather, as follows: 'The world of the senses is certainly a world in which I find myself embedded and to which I belong; it is that world which is explained by natural science in terms of cause and effect. But another world interpenetrates this one, and is regulated by different laws. Each world is subject to its own system of laws.' As long as we are of the opinion that one kind of system of laws could suffice for our world, and that all hangs upon the thread of cause and effect, so long shall we be shrouded in complete illusion.

Only when we can perceive from facts such as the Moon's motion and nutation of the earth's axis that another world extends into this one—only then are we on the right path.

And now, you see, these are the things in which the spiritual and material, as we call them, touch each other, or let us say the soul-world and the material. He who can faithfully observe what is contained within his own self will find the following—and these are things of which humanity must gradually become aware. There are many among you, I imagine, who have already passed the age of 18 years and about 7 months. That was an important moment. Others will have passed twice that number of years—37 years and 2 months—again an important time. After that we have a third very momentous period, 18 years and seven months later, at the age of 55 years and 9 months. Few can notice as yet, not having been trained to do so, the effects and important changes taking place within the individual soul at these times. The nights passed during these periods are the most important nights in an individual's life. It is then that the macrocosm completes its 18 respirations, completes one minute—and we open a window, as it were, facing quite another world. But as I said, people are not yet aware of these points in their lives. Everyone, however, could try to let his mental eye look back over the years he has passed, and if he is over 55 years old to recognize three such important epochs; others two, and most of you at any rate one! In these epochs events take place, which rush up into this world of ours out of quite a different one. Our world opens at these moments to another world.

If we wish to describe this more clearly, we can say that our world is at these times penetrated anew by astral streams; they flow in and out. Of course this really happens every year, but we are here concerned with the 18 years, as they correspond to the 18 respirations per minute. In short, our attention is drawn through the cosmic clock to the breathing of the macrocosm, in which we are embedded. This correspondence with another world, which is manifested through the motion of the moon, is exceptionally important. Because, you see, the world which at these times projects into our own is the very world into which we pass during our sleep, when the ego and the astral body leave our physical and etheric bodies. It must not be thought that the world composing our every-day environment is merely permeated in an abstract way by the astral world; rather should we say, it *breathes in* the astral world, and we can observe the astral in this breathing process through the moon's motion or nutation. You will realize that we have here come to something of great significance. If you remember what I said recently, we may put it in the following way. We have, on the one hand, our world as it is generally observed; and we have in addition, the materialistic superstition that, for instance, if we gaze upwards, we see the sun, a ball of gas, as it is described in books. This is nonsense. The sun is not a ball of gas; but in that place where the sun is, there is something less than empty space—a sucking, absorbing body, in fact, while all around it is that which exerts pressure. Consequently what comes to us from the sun is nothing to do with any product of combustion in the sun, but is a reflection, a raying back of all that the universe has radiated to it.

Where the sun is, is emptier than empty space. This can be said of all parts of the universe where we find ether. For this reason it is so difficult for the physicist to speak of ether, for he thinks that ether is also matter, though more rarefied than ordinary matter. Materialism is still very busy with this perpetual 'rarefying', both the materialism of natural science as well as the materialism of theosophy. It distinguishes first, dense matter; then etheric matter—more rarefied; then astral matter—still more rarefied; and then there is the 'mental' and I do not know what else—always more and more rarefied! The only difference (in this theory of rarefying) between the two forms of materialism is that the one recognizes more degrees of rarefaction than the other. But in the transition from quantifiable matter to ether rarefaction plays no part. Anyone who believes that in ether we have to do merely with a 'rarefying' process is like someone who says: 'I have here a purse full of money; I repeatedly take from it and the money becomes less and less. I take away still more till at last none remains, nothing is left.' But in fact one can continue! The 'nothing' can become less still; for if we get into debt, our money becomes less than nothing. In the same way not only does matter become empty space, but it becomes negative, *less* than nothing—emptier than emptiness; it assumes a 'sucking' nature. Ether is sucking, absorbing. Matter *presses*, ether *absorbs*. The sun is an absorbing, sucking sphere, and wherever ether is present we have this force of suction.

Here we step over into the other aspect of three-dimensional space—we pass from pressure to suction. That which immediately surrounds us in this world, that of which we are constituted as physical and etheric human beings, is both pressing *and* sucking or absorbing. We are a combination of both, whereas the sun possesses the power of suction *only*, being *nothing but ether, nothing but suction*. It is the undulating wave of pressure and suction, ponderable matter and ether, that forms in its alternation a *living* organization. And the living organism continually breathes in the *astral*; the breathing expresses itself through the moon's motion or nutation. And here we begin to divine a second aspect or principle of the world's construction; the one aspect—pressure and suction, physical and etheric; the second—astral. The astral is neither physical nor etheric but is continually inhaled and exhaled; and nutation manifests this.

Now a certain astronomical fact was observed even in most

ancient times. Many thousands of years before the Christian era, the Egyptians knew that after a period of 72 years the fixed stars in their apparent course gain one day on the sun. It seems to us, does it not, that the fixed stars revolve and the sun too revolves, but that the latter revolves more slowly, so that after 72 years the stars are appreciably ahead. This is the reason for the movement of the vernal point (the spring equinoctial point), namely, that the stars move faster. If the spring equinox moves further and further away, the fixed stars must have altered their position in relation to the sun. Briefly, we find that at the end of 72 years the fixed stars are ahead of the sun by one day. For instance, they occupy a particular position on the 30th December, while the *sun* only reaches that point again on the 31st December. The sun has lost a day. After a lapse of 25,920 years this loss is so great, that the sun has described a complete revolution and once again is back at the position we originally noted. We see therefore that in 72 years the sun is one day behind the fixed stars. Now these 72 years are approximately the normal life span of a human being, composed of 25,920 days.

Thus when we multiply 72 years by 360, and consider the human span of life as one day, we have the human life as *one day* of the macrocosm. Man is exhaled, as it were, from the macrocosm, and his life is one day in the macrocosmic year.

So that this revolution, this circle described by the precession of the equinoxes, indicating the macrocosmic year, as already known to the Egyptians thousands of years ago (for they looked upon this period of 72 years as very important), this apparent revolution of the vernal point is connected with man's life and death in the universe—with the life and death, that is, of the macrocosm. And the laws of the life and death of man are something that we must pursue. We have already found how nutation points to another world—as our sense-perception world points to one world, so nutation points to another, the breathing world. And now through what present-day astronomy calls 'precession', we have something we may again call a transition, a transition this time to a state of deep sleep, a transition to still another, a third world. We have thus three worlds, interpenetrating one another, interrelated; but we must not attempt simply to link these worlds in a causal way. Three worlds, a threefold world, as man is a threefold being: one, the world of sense surrounding us, the world we perceive; a second world whose presence is indicated by the motions of the moon; and a third which makes itself known to us by the motion of the equinoctial point, or we might say, by the path of the sun. This third world indeed remains about as unknown to us as the world of our own will is unknown to our ordinary consciousness.

It is important therefore to search everywhere for correspondences between the human microcosm and the macrocosm. And when people of the East, if only in a decadent way, nowadays seek to acquire breathing consciousness, as was done in ancient Oriental wisdom, this is the manifestation of a desire to slip over into this other world—which can otherwise only be recognized through what the moon, so to speak, wills in our world. But in those ancient times, when there was still an ancient wisdom coming to man in a different manner from the way in which we have to seek wisdom nowadays—in those times man also knew how to see this working of inner law in other connections and correspondences.

In the Old Testament the initiates, who were familiar with these matters, always used a certain image or picture—the picture, that is, of the relation between moonlight and sunlight. This we can find also in a certain sense in the Gospels, as I have recently shown you.

We generally speak of moonlight as being reflected sunlight. I am speaking now in the sense of physics, and I shall have to show later on that these expressions are really very inaccurate. In the Old Testament moonlight represented the Jahve or Jehovah power. This power was conceived as a *reflected* power, and the initiates—though not of course the orthodox Rabbis of the Old Testament—knew: the Messiah, the Christ will come, and he will be the *direct* sunlight. Jahve is only his advance reflection. Jahve *is* the sunlight, but not *direct* sunlight. Of course, we are speaking here not of physical sunlight, but of spiritual reality.

Christ entered into human evolution, he who had been present previously only in reflection, in an indirect way in the form of Jehovah. And the need arose to think of the Christ, who lived in Jesus, as the result of a *different* set of laws from those inherent in what a normal perception of nature sees. But if we do not admit this other set of laws, if we believe that the world exists only as the result of cause and effect, then there is no place for the Christ. His place must be prepared by our recognition of three interpenetrating worlds. Then it becomes possible to say: It may be that in this world of sense everything is related through the law of cause and effect as maintained by natural science, but another world permeates this one, and to this other world belongs everything that happened in connection with the Mystery of Golgotha.

In our times, when the desire for an understanding of these matters is becoming more and more manifest, it is important to realize that this understanding must be sought through recognition of these three interpenetrating worlds, which exist simultaneously and are entirely different one from another. This means that we must seek not for one system of laws only, but for *three*; and we must seek for them within ourselves.

If you consider what I have just said, you will see that it will not do to adopt the methods of the Copernican system, and simply draw ellipses intended to show the path of Saturn, Jupiter, Mars, Earth, Venus, Mercury and Sun. That is not what is wanted at all. What is wanted is rather to look at the laws that are active in the worlds that are physically perceptible and see how these laws are interwoven by an altogether different set of laws; and that especially the present moon, in its motion, presents something that is in no way causally connected with the rest of the stellar system, such as would be the case were the moon a part of that system in the same way as other planets. The moon, however, is related to quite another world, which, as it were, interpenetrates ours, and which represents the breathing process of our universe, as the sun represents the interpenetration of our universe by the ether.

Before one engages in astronomy, one must educate oneself in a qualitative sense about planetary motion and inter-dependence in space. For one must be quite clear that sun matter and any other matter—earth matter for instance—can in no circumstances be brought into a simple relationship; because the matter of the sun is, in comparison with the matter of the earth, something absorbing and sucking, while the latter exerts pressure. The motions which express them-selves in nutation are motions proceeding from the astral world, and not from anything that can be found in Newton's principles. It is just this Newtonism that has driven us so far into materialism, because it seizes on the uttermost abstractions. It speaks of a force of gravitation. The sun, it says, attracts the earth, or the earth attracts the moon; a force of attraction exists between these bodies, like some invisible cable. But if really nothing but this force of attraction existed, there would be no cause for the moon to revolve round the earth, or the earth round the sun; the moon would simply fall onto the earth. This would indeed have happened ages ago, if gravitation alone were acting; or the earth would have fallen into the sun. It is therefore quite impossible for us to look to gravitation *alone* for the means of explaining the imagined or actual motions of celestial bodies. So what do they do? Let us see! Here we have a planet imbued with a constant desire to fall into the sun—supposing we were to have the law of gravitation alone. But now we will suppose that this planet has at some time or other been given another force, a tangential force. This impetus acts with such and such a power, and the force of gravitation acts at the same time with such and such a power, so that eventually the planet does not fall into the sun, but has to move along a line resulting from both forces.

You see that Newton's theory finds it necessary to assume some kind of original impetus, some kind of first push in the case of each planet, of each moving celestial body. There must always be some extra-mundane God somewhere, who gives this impetus, who imparts this tangential force. This is always presupposed; and remember, this assumption was made at a time when we had lost all idea of bringing the material and the spiritual into any kind of connection, when we were incapable of conceiving of anything but a perfectly external 'push'.

Here we have an instance of the inability of materialism to understand matter. I have repeatedly drawn your attention to this of late. It follows that materialism is therefore also unable to understand the *motions* of matter, and is compelled to give quite an anthropomorphic explanation of them, picturing God as a being with wholly human attributes, who simply gives the moon a push and the earth a push. The earth and moon then 'attract' each other—and behold, from these two forces, the push and the attraction, we have their movements in the heavens.

It is from ideas of this kind that the solar system is constructed today. But to get a real understanding of the universe it is absolutely necessary to look for the connection between what lives in man, and what lives in the macrocosm. For man is truly a microcosm in the macrocosm. Of this we will speak further tomorrow.

Lecture 5

Our studies of the last few days will have made it clear to you that it is altogether impossible to look upon the configuration of the spatial universe and its movements in the way adopted by modern science. For not only is the universe regarded as entirely separate from man, but even the separate celestial bodies, which appear to our sight as disconnected from each other, are each treated as isolated bodies; and then, in their isolation, their effects upon each other are observed. This is like studying the human organism by examining first an arm and then a leg, in order afterwards to understand the complete organism from the way in which the single members work together. But you can't actually comprehend the human organism by studying its separate parts—all investigation of the human body must have its starting point in the *whole*, from which we can then proceed to the separate parts.

The same applies to the solar system, and also to the solar system in its relation to the whole visible stellar universe. For the sun, moon, earth and other planets are only parts of the whole system. Why should the sun, for instance, be considered as an isolated body? There is absolutely no reason why we should imagine the sun to be merely just where we see it, limited by the boundaries within which our eyes perceive it. In this connection the philosopher Schelling was quite correct when he declined to ask the question 'Where is the sun?' with any other meaning than 'Where is its influence felt?' If the sun acts upon the earth, the effects of such activity must necessarily belong to the sphere of the sun; and it is very wrong to extract a part from a whole and study that part by itself. But this is the very thing modern materialistic conceptions of the universe have set out to do, and their influences have grown stronger and stronger ever since the middle of the fifteenth century. This is what Goethe always fought against in his scientific investigations, and against which all true followers of his science must also fight. Goethe found himself compelled to draw attention to the fact that we must not study nature without man, without keeping in mind the relation of nature to man. The study of natural phenomena outside man must be underpinned by an understanding of man's nature.

The following example will show you the value of some of the assertions made by modern astronomy. Modern astronomy endeavours, with all manner of arguments, to speak of an elliptic path of the earth around the sun. It asserts that this motion was first initiated by that tangential propulsion of which I spoke yesterday in connection with the sun's gravitational attraction. But astronomy cannot, and does not, deny the fact that when speaking of attraction, not only does the sun attract the earth, but the earth must also attract the sun. This, however, obliges us to conclude that we cannot speak of an elliptical orbit of the earth around the sun, for if the attraction be mutual we cannot have a one-sided motion of the earth around the sun, but both of them must revolve round a neutral point. In other words, this orbit cannot take place in a manner that would allow us to look on the sun's centre as the pivot, but the pivot must be a neutral point situated between the centre of the sun and the centre of the earth. In telling you this I am not raising objections to astronomy, I am merely telling you what you can find for yourselves in astronomical books. Thus we are compelled to admit the existence—somehow or other—of a pivot between the two spheres.

Our astronomy consoles itself by maintaining that this pivot or point lies within the sun itself. Both earth and sun, then, revolve around this point. And so, once again, we get no direct revolution of earth round sun, but the sun also revolves, revolving however around a point lying within itself. Thus ordinary astronomy has come so far as to assume as pivot a point that is not the centre of the sun, but lies in the line connecting the sun and the earth, yet is still within the sun. But now we are confronted with another difficulty. The size of the sun has first to be calculated. (The truth of the above assumption depends upon the calculated size of the sun.) Upon the result of such calculation is built a conclusion which must of course possess a certain limited validity (the calculations being made from evidence of the senses), but which need not necessarily be the criterion by which we judge what truly underlies nature's phenomena.

Thus it is necessary to keep a strict eye upon modern astronomy, as well as on other sciences, in order to discern the places—and they are numerous—where science overreaches itself, and gets into difficulties.

This difficulty cannot be settled by studying the outer aspect of the phenomena; we can only arrive at a true result by examining the universe in its relation to man. We must, in the first place, take note of the previously explained connections between the universe and man; and then we must add a good many other facts, before we can produce a perfectly true world-picture. We have said before that we must imagine, first of all, ordinary ponderable matter—matter that can be weighed. Light we cannot weigh; it does not belong to the realm of ponderable matter, and neither does warmth (heat). First then, we must imagine the ponderable, then we must contrast this with the ether. We said it is wrong to consider the sun as consisting of ponderable matter like the earth's matter. The sun is something which is actually less than space—so to speak, a vacuum of space; it is something that *sucks in*, in contrast to the *pressure* exerted by ponderable matter.

And we have to do not only with an accumulation (in the sun) of this absorbent ether in the outer universe, but also with the fact that this ether is distributed far and wide. Everywhere we find, co-existing with the force of pressure, the absorbent force of suction. We ourselves carry this force of suction in our own etheric bodies.

This comprises all that we call space. Pressure and suction—these two, we find in space. But not only do we possess our *physical* body, composed of ponderable matter which it assimilates and again expels, not only have we also an *etheric* body, composed of absorbent ether, but we have in addition an *astral* body—if we may use the term 'body' in this connection. What does the possession of this third body imply? It means that we have within us something that is no longer spatial, though it has a certain relation to space. This relationship can be proved when we realize that during waking hours the astral body interpenetrates the etheric and physical bodies. But the etheric body acts very differently when we are awake and when we are asleep. A different relation is established between the etheric and physical bodies when we wake, and this is caused by the astral body. It is active, and works upon the spatial, though it is not itself spatial. It brings order and organization into the correlations of space. This organizing activity of the astral body within us takes place also in the outer universe, where it manifests in the following way.

Try for the moment to consider space alone, and out of the whole visible heavens let us consider the regions that comprise the zodiac. I do not intend here to deal in detail with the various zodiacal signs, but let us consider the directions to which we look in the heavens when we turn, for instance, towards Aries (Ram) in the zodiac; then Taurus, Gemini, Cancer, Leo, Virgo, Libra, Scorpio, Sagittarius, Capricorn, Aquarius and Pisces. All we have to note, in the first place, is that the space that lies before us as our visible universe is divided in this way. The signs merely denote the boundary of a certain section of space.

Now we must not imagine that these directions of space can

be treated in such a manner that one might say: 'There is empty space, and I just draw a line somewhere into it.' Such a thing as mathematics calls 'space' simply does not exist; but everywhere are *lines of force, directions of force*, and these are not equal, they vary, they are differentiated. We can distinguish between these twelve regions by realizing that if we turn in the direction of the sign Aries, the force we experience is a different one than it would be had we faced the sign Libra or Cancer. In each direction the force differs. Man will not admit this as long as he lives merely in the world of the senses; but as soon as he ascends to the imaginative life of the soul, he no longer experiences the directions in space as the same when facing Aries or Cancer, but feels their influence upon him as greatly differentiated.

To give you a parallel, I might present the following to you. Imagine that you arrange round you a circle of twelve persons in such a manner that those most sympathetic to you occupy one part of the circle, then come the less sympathetic, until on the other side you have all those who are antipathetic to you. (We are not imagining the degree of sympathy or antipathy to result from any personal emotion; it may be merely a matter of outward appearances.) Now if you turn round within the circle, twelve pictures pass before your vision, and at the same time you experience a graduated series of differentiated sensations. Man becomes aware of such a series of sensations if, after attaining to imaginative perception, he moves around within the zodiac. A similar gradation of sensation, a similar gradation of vision is produced in him, and it takes place within him the moment he escapes from the lack of differentiation of ordinary sense-existence. So when we are dealing with these various sections of space there is no sameness, for we must realize that each of these directions exerts a different influence upon us.

You see, here a fact comes to light which is intimately connected with man's whole evolution. Had he remained at the stage of ancient consciousness, atavistic picture-consciousness, he would still strongly experience the reality of this differentiation in the various sections of the heavens; he would have been conscious of a sensation of sympathy towards one direction of space and antipathy towards another. Man has however been torn away from this play of forces which at one time surrounded him; he has been extracted from it because his present organization has placed him into the sense-world. But the fact that man is really organized in accordance with cosmic laws can even now be proved, and by quite external experiments, if attention is paid to certain phenomena. For it is by no means mere nonsense to say that certain sicknesses can be cured more quickly if the patient's bed is placed in an east-west alignment. It is no superstition but a fact capable of definite proof. But this is not intended as a recommendation to each of you to place your bed in a certain position! I have had so many experiences of this kind that I feel it necessary to interject a word of warning here! In Berlin, for instance, at the end of an anthroposophical discourse, I once said there was a certain value in being able to put on my goloshes when it was raining, without sitting down, and that this could be done by first standing upon one leg and then upon the other; and I added, 'And one ought to be able to stand upon one leg!' Later, on returning from London to Berlin, I found that this had led to members of the Anthroposophical Society there being recommended, as esoteric training, to stand upon one leg for a short time at midnight! Many assertions made about us, you see, start from such things. Time and again things of this sort get said and then find their way into this or that newspaper article through the pen of some well- or ill-disposed person—generally the latter. So I repeat, I have no wish at all to recommend that each of you place his bed in one particular position. Nevertheless, this fact and many others show that even today, in the inner or subconscious part of our being, we still stand in a certain relation to these exterior spatial differentiations into which we have been placed.

But how do we possess these relationships? We possess them through the astral body, which creates them. They are only possible to us because our astral body places us into the astral world, a world which though acting upon space is not itself spatial. We only conceive the zodiac in its full meaning when we regard it as representative of the astral world beyond.

And now, without considering modern astronomical theories, let us examine these phenomena which appear to our sense of vision. We know that either actually or apparently the sun passes through the zodiac in various ways; in its daily course, in its yearly course, and again in its course through the Platonic year, through the precession of the equinoxes. This points to the fact that the effects upon us of that absorbent ether ball the sun vary greatly, as they come from the different directions of space. At one time the sun's workings affect us from a part of space we call Aries, at another time from a different part and so on.

Taking the case of an inhabitant of our own part of the globe, we can see that at any given time one half of the zodiacal signs face him, while the other half is obscured by the earth. In other words, in relation to this differentiation of space, we are turned directly towards the one part of the zodiac while between the other part and ourselves stands the earth. Obviously this has nothing whatever to do with either an actual or an apparent motion; it is a simple fact that at any given moment we face one part of the zodiac, while the earth comes between us and the other part. Now please try to imagine these sections of space with our earth obscuring some of them. What does it mean for us? It is plain that the one half will influence us directly, the other not directly, but rather, shall I say, through its absence. At one time we have the direct working of these differentiated regions of space, at another time the working of their absence—the effect, as it were, of their non-presence. This fact is something which is *active* within us and enables us to some extent to bring into a kind of relationship what is working directly upon us and what is absent, from whose direct influence we are removed, for it opens up another possibility.

Let us say that a certain kind of influence proceeds from the direction of the sign Cancer. This would be opposed by an influence from Capricorn, but the latter is taken away, is intercepted. Consequently I have in me the influence of Cancer and opposed to it the intercepted Capricornian influence; the influence of Cancer thereby gains entry to me in a sense, is given me to make something of. Of course, that which is absent cannot act upon me in the same way as that which is present; but I gain a certain influence upon the sign that acts upon me through the opposition exerted by its intercepted antithesis. Through the fact that I stand upon the earth the celestial influences become quite different to what they would be, were I hovering freely in space and directly exposed to them all.

I want you to note this point specially, and then you will realize that you cannot simply say: Above us we have the signs Aries, Pisces, Aquarius, etc., and below Libra, Virgo, and so on, but you will have to conceive the whole as a kind of organization, with yourself harnessed into it. And as you progress, on account of the earth's revolution, from sign to sign, you are being carried through all these direct influences in turn. Here at one point, the Scorpio influence was taken away from you, and there at another point you are carried into it. An analogy is the taking of food; you were hungry, the food was not there within you, but after the meal the food is present within you. The Scorpio influence was absent here, but at this other point became active. And so we form connections with the surrounding cosmos as we come into different relations with it through the earth's movement. But are we conscious of these varying influences, while yet on the physical plane? No, we are not; we have seen that the physical world withdraws us from them. But the moment our astral body and ego withdraw from our physical and etheric bodies, we find ourselves within these forces; they act directly and strongly upon us. These extra-earthly, heavenly influences then affect that part of us no longer connected with the physical and etheric as powerfully as food upon the physical body. It is just this descent into the physical that is the cause of our withdrawal from these celestial influences. We may therefore consider the astral body as being in a sense part of the celestial, and not of the terrestrial universe, for when, together with the ego, it is outside the physical body, we have to ascribe it to non-terrestrial influences.

By considering the matter in this way, we are gradually brought to the conclusion that man becomes receptive to these celestial forces in so far as he ceases to act through the organs of his physical body—that is to say, when he is, through this non-activity, more or less in a state of sleep. Children are always more or less asleep, therefore the child is much more receptive to celestial influences than an adult. As we grow up we work our way further and further into earthly conditions. During childhood, all that is within the skin is still plastic and in a state of formation. The formative powers become less and less active with the years, until, at a con-siderably later point in life, they become very much dimin-ished. This shows that the inward-directed formation process stands in a certain relation to the movements and configura-tions of the outer celestial universe. But the part of our being which, as far as consciousness is concerned, remains in a continuous state of sleep—such as our heart-activity, our digestive processes, etc., in fact all the inner physical pro-cesses—all this part of our being remains under the influences of the super-physical during the whole of our life. (These processes are induced in the same way as is the process that goes on when I take a step forward consciously, only they are all directed inward instead of outward.)

Let us take a characteristic example. By means of the inner movements of the intestines the chyme is propelled on its path. These are internal movements within the boundary of the human skin, and therefore, as we have said, dependent upon what is beyond the earth. Fundamentally, man as such is dependent upon the terrestrial, upon ponderable-terrestrial matter, only as far as things outside his skin are concerned. But the moment any *outer* act or circumstance is translated into activity within the skin, then there begins in his organism an activity that is related to the supersensible.

When you take a piece of sugar into the palm of your hand, you feel its weight physically, you raise it to your lips; the process is still physical. But as soon as you dissolve it on the tongue and it enters the sphere of taste, it no longer remains within the scope of earthly processes but becomes subject to forces from beyond the earth.

In order to find the working of the super-earthly, we must penetrate into what is enclosed within the human skin. This will lead you to realize that while you go about in the world, bearing with you, as it were, your whole self, you are in the realm of the earthly. But as soon as you penetrate within, even only into your physical organization, you are no longer in the realm of the earthly, but have entered a sphere dependent upon super-earthly forces. You can easily prove for yourselves the fact that within you resides something that is not subsumed within purely earthly existence, if you recall the oft-repeated fact that the human brain floats in the meningeal fluid. If this were not the case, the pressure of the brain upon the floor of the skull would crush all the blood vessels. Any text book dealing with such matters will tell you the weight of the brain. If you read Bischoff, for instance, you will notice he asserts that the female brain is much lighter than that of a male—an assertion rendered absurd later on, to the delight of the ladies, when it was found upon examination that the brain of Bischoff himself proved to be a good deal less in weight than the lightest of the female brains examined by him. I only mention this in passing, as an example of the general value of human judgements.

The human brain, however, possessing as it does a considerable weight—at least 1,200 to 1,300 grams—does not exert a pressure anything like commensurate with its actual weight, but only a weight of comparatively few grammes, because of the meningeal fluid. You remember the law of Archimedes, according to which the weight of an object is reduced by the weight of the water it displaces. Therefore the pressure of the brain is equal to only a few grammes because it floats in fluid. If it pressed downwards with its full weight, we could not use our brain for thinking. It overcomes its weight because it floats in fluid. We do not think with the matter of the brain, but with that which withdraws itself from the matter, with the upward striving forces, with what grows beyond the earth. And we must observe this in all parts of our organization. Just as we withdraw ourselves inwardly from the forces of terrestrial gravity in the case of the weight of the brain (not in an outer sense, of course, for the brain upon the scales shows its full weight, even while within us), so do we similarly sever ourselves from earthly physical and chemical forces of other kinds.

What enables us to sever ourselves from these forces? It is the ego and the astral body. As soon as these act upon the etheric and physical bodies in such a way as to withdraw the etheric from the physical, the absorbent force of suction is then absent, and only ponderable matter remains. Our ponderable form is not part of the earth, for the earth does not sustain it in its original form, but destroys it. The earth-forces do not contain in them what gives man his form. That is not difficult to comprehend, for we have seen that we sever ourselves inwardly from earth-forces. All that our astral body and ego endow us with, relates us to forces that are active beyond the earth.

Our next question must be: What is the nature of this relation? To ascertain this, we must in a certain way study the whole quality and nature of man. We find in the first place his complete *form* or *figure*. I do not mean by this the form which I would draw if I were to make a sketch of him, but man's whole configuration and organization. This would include, for example, the fact that the eyes are situated in the face, and the heels on the feet; for this is part of the inner laws at work in man's form.

Expressionistic painters may assert that the human being could be drawn in such a way that his toe takes the place of his nose, or that one eye is placed here and the other in his hand. Yes, there really are such people, but they only show how little inner relationship they have with the world. These days materialistic thought has got as far as being able to depict single things *separately*, when they really belong together with the whole and ought not to be depicted in isolation.

Firstly therefore, we have man's complete *form*; and this, as you know very well, is not produced as a carved wooden figure is produced, but is formed from within. We cannot even re-carve any part that does not happen to meet with our approval. The human form is modelled by forces residing within our skin—and these are forces from beyond the earth. Therefore when we contemplate a human form, we are looking at a super-earthly creation.

Secondly we can distinguish in man, apart from his form, all that comes under the category of *internal motion*. Take, for instance, the blood and the other bodily juices; these possess internal motion, which is also produced from within, is, so to speak, situated even deeper in us than our form. The latter presses forward to the periphery, while internal motion takes place entirely within; and it is again a process that stands in relation with the world that is beyond the earth.

Thirdly, *the activity of the organs.* Organs such as the lungs, liver, spleen, etc., are responsible for something within us I refer to as a third aspect.

Consider for example an important organ, the heart, of which I have recently often spoken. We realize that in a certain sense the heart has been woven together. By pursuing embryology, we find how the heart is gradually woven together or configured, as it were, by blood circulation, and is not a primary form. And it is the same with other organs. They are the *results* of these circulations, rather than the causes of them. Within the organs circulation comes to a standstill, in certain respects, undergoes a kind of metamorphosis, and proceeds further in a different way. To illustrate the idea, let us say we have a stream of water falling over a rock. It throws up a variety of water formations and then flows on. These formations are caused by the forces of equilibrium and motion at this place. Now imagine that suddenly all this were to petrify; a skin would be formed like a wall, then the rest would flow on again, leaving behind the form of an organic structure. We should have the current passing through the structure, coming out again and flowing on further in an altered form. You can imagine something like this in the case of the flow of blood, as it circulates through the heart. I can only indicate these things here. They are well-founded, but only an indication of them can be given here.

The way organs are formed depends upon the flow of inner forces, yet they are also something within us that comes into relation with what is outside. We have here something which, as you can see from an example I will give, stands in closer relation with the earthly; through these organs we are brought from the interior into contact with the exterior.

Take the case of the lungs. The lungs are internal organs which are at the same time the basis of respiration. As the instrument for the transmutation of inhaled oxygen into exhaled carbonic acid, the lungs form a relation with something that has significance for man, but yet exists outside him in the realm of the earthly. In this way we return, as it were, to the terrestrial environment via internal organic activities. The moment we pass, through organic activity, beyond the boundary of our skin, we are outside in the terrestrial sphere. You see, all these processes that take place entirely within us, the formation and regulation of fluidic movements, etc., stand in a relationship with what is super-earthly; whereas when we come to the organs we again approach the terrestrial. Here we have the union of heaven and earth in man. The lungs are *built up* by the super-earthly, but what they *do* with the oxygen brings them into relation with the earthly. And when man takes up still more earthly substances and receives them into his organism, he comes into immediate contact, through the process of *metabolism*, with the truly earthly.

Thus we can study man from four different points of view: *complete* or overall *form*, in so far as this is built up from within outwards, *internal motion, organic activity* and *metabolism*. If we study the overall form, which arises entirely through inner forces, we find that it has the least connection of all with the earthly. This point will be further explained tomorrow. We only begin to gain an understanding of such connection when we relate, as we shall do tomorrow, the complete form of man to the *zodiac*. The inner motion, the circulation of the blood, lymph, etc., can only be conceived in their reality when related to our *planetary system*. And when we come to the activity of the organs, we are already *approaching the terrestrial*.

I gave you the example of the lungs, which, in respect to their internal structure, are formed by cosmic forces, but where they take in oxygen, come into relation with the air. Other human organs come into relation with water, others again with heat, etc. Therefore, in studying the activity of the organs, we come into contact with the world of the elements—with fire, water, air. Only when our observations are centred upon actual assimilation, or metabolism, are we in the sphere of the earth. The world of elements encompasses the earth as the sphere of water and air, and only when we encounter the process of metabolism do we approach our actual relationship with the earth itself.

In this way we can discover our relationship to the universe surrounding us:

Zodiac:	(1)	Overall form
World of the planets:	(2)	Internal motion
World of the elements:	(3)	Activity of the organs
Earth:	(4)	Metabolism

And now consider, if we understand the human form in all its nature and conditions, and find the possibility of tracing it back to the zodiac—that is, to the world of fixed stars—then and then only are we able to form, *from man*, an idea of all that is visible to us in surrounding space; for it cannot be investigated by mechanical or mathematical means, but only through gaining knowledge of man's complete form. Neither are planetary motions to be examined merely by means of a telescope. With a telescope one merely finds their positions— setting it first to one star and then to the other, finding the angle, and in this way discovering the positions. What is actually present is something that is formed from within outwards, which in other words corresponds to processes of the planetary world. It is by a study of the activities and effects of man's bodily fluids and circulation that we shall learn to understand the planetary activities. Similarly, if we comprehend our own organic activities, we shall also understand what goes on in the world of the elements; and when we are able to understand what happens in man at the moment when earthly substance is introduced into his metabolic system, we shall be able to distinguish and spatially separate earthly influences from all other super-earthly influences.

Lecture 6

We have seen that we must search for a harmony between the processes taking place in man and the processes that take place in the outer universe. Let us once again recall briefly the point to which our studies led us yesterday. We said that man had to be regarded, to begin with, from four points of view. Firstly, in relation to the forces responsible for his form; secondly in relation to all the forces expressing themselves in the circulation of the blood, lymph, etc., in short the forces of internal motion. (In the fully-grown adult, as you know, the formative forces are to a large extent in a state of rest, whereas forces of motion are in a state of continual flow.) Thirdly, we have the organic forces; and fourthly, metabolism as such.

To begin with we must consider all that relates to the formative forces. These are the forces which work outward from within until they reach the outermost periphery, the limits of our circumference. If we formed a silhouette of man, seen as it were from all sides, we should comprehend and encompass the furthest extent of these inner forces, which build him up from within outwards.

Now it should not be difficult to understand that these structuring forces must be connected with other forces, which, like them, are active at our periphery and are to be discovered there. These are the forces active in the senses. The senses of man lie, as you know, upon his external periphery. They are of course distributed over it and differentiated, but in order to come into contact with the forces acting in the senses you must look for them at the periphery, and this justifies us in saying that the formative forces must have a connection with the activity of the senses. We shall perhaps understand this point better if we remember the words that Goethe quotes, as uttered by one of the old mystics.

Were the eye not sun-like in itself,
How could we see the sun?

Now it cannot be the light-activity surrounding us all the time that is meant when the eye is said to be sun-like or light-like, for this light-activity can be perceived by the eye only when the eye is completely formed. It cannot therefore be this that is meant, when we are speaking of the building up of the eye through light. We must imagine this light-activity as something intrinsically different. We actually arrive at a certain conception of this by following man during the time between death and a new birth. For during this period his experiences consist in part—but of course, only in part—in a perception of the gradual transformation of the forces within him from the preceding physical life to the new one; and he perceives how the limb-forces are transformed in the time between death and a new birth into the head-form. These experiences are no less rich in content than are those experiences we live through in this life, when we watch the gradual quickening of the plants in spring and their decay in autumn, etc.

All this building up that goes on in man in the time between death and re-birth is a great wealth of events, a wealth of real happenings which are by no means so easy to grasp as the mere abstract idea of them. All that takes place during this time to effect the transformation of the forces of our limbs into those of the head for the new incarnation is extraordinarily manifold. Man himself partakes in the process. He experiences, for instance, something akin to the *building up of the eye*. But he does not experience it in the same manner as he did during the long evolutionary period, when he passed through the various evolutionary stages preceding our current Earth stage, namely, those of Moon, Sun and Saturn. The forces of the stellar universe then acted upon him in a different way. This stellar universe was also differently formed from the way it is now.

It is of great importance to form clear ideas on these matters. If we consider our present perceptions of what is around us, what are they? They are really pictures. Behind these pictures, of course, lies the real world; but the world underlying these pictures is what actually built up man before he had evolved sufficiently to be able to perceive them. Today we perceive with our eyes images of the surrounding world. Behind these lies what has built up our eyes. So we can say that if the forces underlying our image of the sun had not constructed the eye, the eye could not perceive this image of the sun.

Thus, you see, we have to somewhat modify what Goethe says; for while the perception of light nowadays produces images, what first built up the sense-organs at our periphery were not images but *realities*. So that when we look around us in this world, what we perceive are really the forces that have built us up—our own formative forces. They have now drawn into us; that which acted from without up to the Earth period of evolution, now works from within.

We will retain this thought for our succeeding studies and will now bring together the first and fourth of these forces.

1. Structuring forces
2. Forces of inner movement
3. Organic forces
4. Assimilative, or metabolic forces

Let us, for the moment, consider the last named. The process of metabolism has already become somewhat irregular in the human being but there are natural causes which still lead us to hold to a certain regularity in this respect; and you all know that a certain disorder results if, for some reason or other, we are prevented from establishing a rhythmic metabolism. We can deviate from it within limits, but we always endeavour to return again to a certain rhythm; and you know that this rhythm is one of the first essentials of physical health. It is a rhythm that embraces day and night. The rhythmic process of metabolism is completed in 24 hours. Twenty-four hours after breakfast you again have an appetite for breakfast. All that is connected with assimilation is connected also with the day's rhythmic course. I would now ask you to compare the solidity, the firmness of the exterior periphery of your body with the mobility of the forces of assimilation. One can say that no alterations take place in the former, while assimilation repeats itself every 24 hours. A great deal takes place inside your organism, but your periphery remains unchanged. Now try to discover, in the outer world, something corresponding with this inner mobility in relation to firmness, that you find in man. Look at the universe of stars. Note how the constellations move as little as do the features on the surface of the human exterior. You will find that the constellation of Aries is always at a fixed distance from the constellation of Taurus, just as your two eyes remain at the same distance from one another. But *apparently* this *whole* stellar heaven moves; apparently it revolves around the earth. Well, people are no longer ignorant about this nowadays; they know that the movement is merely apparent, and ascribe its appearance to a revolution of the earth upon its own axis.

Many have been the attempts to find proof for this revolution of the earth on its own axis. It was really only during the fifties of the last century that people established the right to speak of such a revolution, for it was only then that the pendulum experiments of Foucault demonstrated how this turning of the earth occurs. I will not go into this further today. However, this gave us valid proof of a process which repeats itself every 24 hours. In relation to the fixed constellations, it provides an analogy of the rhythmic course of our metabolism compared to the fixed nature of our exterior form; and you can find, if you examine thoroughly all the conditions and relationships, precise evidence for the earth's movement in the processes of our metabolism.

In our day, you see, there are various so-called theories of relativity which claim that we cannot really speak of absolute motion. If I look out of the window of a railway carriage and think that the objects outside are moving, in reality it is the train and myself that are moving. But strictly speaking one cannot prove that the world outside is not also moving in an opposite direction! All this kind of talk is, as a matter of fact, of little value. For if one person walks towards another who stands still while the first approaches him, it is, *relatively* speaking, immaterial whether he says: 'I approach him' or 'he approaches me'. Looked at in this way there seems to be no difference. As you know, such considerations form the foundations of Einstein's theories of relativity.

Yet there is a way in which one can strictly *prove* the motion, for the person who remains still will not experience fatigue, whereas the one who walks will do so. Thus inner processes can demonstrate the absolute reality of motion; indeed there are no other proofs but inner processes. Applying this to the earth, we can truly speak there too of absolute motion, for spiritual science enables us to realize that this motion is the equivalent of the inner motion of metabolism as compared with the fixed form of man. We should not lay so much stress upon the fact that the earth rotates round its axis and thereby brings about an apparent solar motion in space, but should instead relate this terrestrial motion to the whole starry universe; we should not speak of sun days, but rather of star days—which are not synonymous, for the stellar day is shorter that the solar. A correction is always necessary in formulae dealing with the solar day. Hence we can truly speak of this movement of the earth on its axis as of something that can be derived from the nature of man himself; for as already pointed out, the inner motion of metabolism within us relates to our outer form in the same way as the earth's rotation relates to the fixed stars, as embodied in the zodiac.

When we look at the zodiac, it is the outer, cosmic representative of our own outer form. When we consider the earth, we have before us the embodiment of assimilative forces within us; and in each case there is a corresponding relation of movement.

Now it will be a little more difficult to find the relationship between (2) and (3), between inner movement and organic forces. We can however make the matter comprehensible in the following way. If you consider the inner movements within the human organism, you will readily conclude that they are something not in the least fixed, as his outer, peripheral shape is. They are in motion. But something further is connected with this movement. The movements include that of the blood as well as the nerve-fluid, lymph, etc. We need not give a detailed list of them here, but there are seven of these inner movements. Connected with these movements are the individual organs. These motions integrate the organs in the course of their flow; in the latter we must recognize the results of these motions. On many recent occasions I have drawn attention to the real truth about the human heart. The materialistic view of the world, as I have pointed out, believes the heart to be a kind of pump, forcing blood through the whole body. But this is not the case; on the contrary, the pulsation of the heart is not the cause but the *effect* of circulation. Organ functions are integrated into the living flow of inner motions.

If we try to discover a cosmic equivalent for this, we will find it by observing the movements of the planets, especially if we consider their motions in relation to the movements of the moon. You will know—for I have often spoken of this—about the connection between lunar motion and the phenomena of the tides; and much more besides is connected with this lunar motion. Were we to study the phenomena of nature more deeply, we should find that not only does *light* appear as a result of the sunrise, but other—and indeed more material—effects in our earth-environment are connected with planetary motion. Once this comes to be the basis of real, genuine study, we shall realize the harmony existing between many phenomena on the earth and the motions of the planets. We shall study the effects of planetary influence upon air, water and earth, in the same way as we study—in the human body—the influences upon their respective organs of the forces of inner movement in the circulation of the blood, and in other circulations. In this way we shall discover a certain reciprocal action between organic activities and planetary movement. Just as we have already observed a correspondence between earth and the fixed stars, so now we shall in fact have before us a similar correspondence between the elements of earth, water, air, fire (heat) and the planets—among which we reckon, of course, the sun.

Thus we arrive at a certain relation between occurrences within the human organism and those taking place outside in the macrocosm. For the present, however, we need concern ourselves only with the organic forces. How are they built up in the human body? They are built up in such a manner that as we follow human life during the periods of this building-up process of the organs, we may recognize with a fair degree of accuracy that the process is related to the course of the year, in the same way as metabolism is related to the course of the day. Observe how this forming, structuring process takes place in the child, commencing at conception and proceeding until he first 'sees the light of day' as it is beautifully expressed. After this, and especially during the first months after birth, the building-up process proceeds still further—over the course of a year in fact. Then we have another period of about one year, up to the appearance of the first teeth. Thus, in the building process of the organs we have a yearly course. But this course stands in a similar relation to the forces of inner movement in us as changing seasonal conditions—spring, summer, autumn and winter—do to the planets. Here again we discover something in us that has correspondences in the macrocosm. We cannot study these matters in any other way than by comparing their specific details. All I can do today is to draw your attention to certain facts that bear upon this subject, for were we to examine the connections in detail it would take us too long; but the more carefully you study certain relationships in the human being during the actual building process of the organs, and see them in connection with the forces of inner movement, the more you will discover this harmony and interaction. Once the organs are fully developed, the human being extricates himself from these forces. By observing these things, and their connection with inner forces of movement, you will find analagous relationships with the connection between the seasons and planetary movements. But we must avoid basing these observations upon the idea of the heart being a pump; on the contrary, the heart must be viewed as a creation of the circulation of the blood. We must, so to speak, integrate the heart into a living blood-circulation. The movement of the sun too must be thought of as similarly integrated into the movements of the planets. An unbiased examination of conditions inside us compels us to speak of a rotation of the earth on her axis causing an apparent motion of the starry heavens—for this is equivalent to the motions of metabolism in their relationship to our human outer form. But we cannot speak of a movement of the earth around the sun during the year. We cannot do this, if we understand what occurs within us, which lives in close connection with the macrocosm; for we must not conceive of that which moves towards the heart in any other manner than we would the other flows of movement within us. We must therefore recognize that we are concerned not with an elliptical movement of the earth in the course of the year but rather with a movement which corresponds to the solar motion. That is, earth and sun *move together* in the course of the year; the one does not circle around the other. The latter opinion is the result of judging things by outer appearances; what we actually have here is the motion of both these bodies in space with a certain connection between the two. This is something in Copernican theory that will have to be substantially corrected. But there is yet another way in which we must conceive man's relationship with macro-cosmic nature.

What is the real nature of the process which we observe in the daily movement of metabolism? Only part of this process occurs while we are conscious, another part being accomplished while consciousness is excluded, while the ego and astral body are separated from the physical and etheric. Now we must especially note the following. We do not experience *in the same way* what takes place between waking and going to sleep and what takes place between going to sleep and waking. Just consider the relation between the two moments of time— going to sleep and waking. If you do this with an unprejudiced mind, you will arrive at an unequivocal view of this matter. When you go to sleep, you are, as it were, at the zero point of your being; the condition of sleep is not merely one of rest, it is the opposite of the waking state. At the moment of waking you are really in the same relation to yourself and your environment as at the moment of going to sleep. The one is the equivalent of the other, the only difference being that of *direction*. Awaking means passing from sleep to the waking state; falling asleep is the reverse. Apart from direction they are absolutely alike. Therefore if we could indicate the movements of metabolism by a line, then it cannot be a straight line or a circle, for they would not contain the points of awaking and of falling asleep. We must find a line which actually depicts the movements of metabolism, so as to contain these points, and the only one—search as long as you like—is the lemniscate. Here you have the point of awaking in one direction and the point of falling asleep in the other direction. The directions alone are opposite, the two points being equal conditions. We can now distinguish in a real way the cycle of day and the cycle of night.

Where does all this lead us? If we have grasped the fact that the motion of our daily metabolism corresponds to the motion of the earth, we can no longer attribute a merely circular motion to it (diagram). On the contrary, we must see that the earth actually proceeds along its path in a way that produces a lemniscate line. The motion is not a simple revolution, but a more complicated movement; each point of the terrestrial surface describes a lemniscate, which is also the line described by the metabolic process.

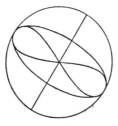

We cannot therefore imagine the earth's movement to consist merely of a rotation on its axis, for in reality it is a complicated motion in which every point upon which you stand describes a lemniscate—actually *in order* to form the foundation for the movement of your metabolic processes. It is absolutely necessary to seek in the movements of the outer universe the equivalent of movements taking place within us. For only by studying the changes within our bodies can we arrive at an understanding of the planetary motions exterior to us. When a person uses his limbs to move and *becomes tired*, we cannot go on arguing the point as to whether he is in relative or actual motion! It is out of the question to say: Perhaps the movement is only relative, perhaps the other man whom he is approaching is after all really approaching him! Theories of relativity no longer hold water when our inner motion *proves* that we move. And in fact the only way to prove the movements in the interior of the earth is by means of the inner changes that go on within us. The movements of metabolism, for example, are the true reflection of the movements which earth executes in space. And again, what we have termed the organ-building forces, active in the course of the year, are the equivalent of the annual motion of earth and sun together. We shall have occasion to speak more specifically of these things later.

Now all this will make it clear that we can certainly speak of a daily rotation of the earth around its axis, but by no means of a yearly motion of the earth around the sun. For the earth follows the sun, describing the same path.

Various other facts show that we have no right to speak of such an orbit around the sun. To give one instance, this is clear from the fact that it was found necessary—I have spoken of this before—simply to suppress one statement by Copernicus. Were the earth revolving round the sun, we should of course expect her axis, which owing to its inertia remains parallel, to point in the direction of different fixed stars during this revolution. But it does not! If the earth revolved round the sun, the axis could not continually point in the direction of the Pole-star, for the point indicated would itself have to revolve round the Pole-star; it does not however do this, the axis continually points to the Pole-star. That line, which if the theory were true would visibly correspond to the progressive motion of the earth in its relation to the sun, is not to be found. It is in a spiral, screw-like path that the earth follows the sun, boring its way, as it were, into cosmic space.

I have already indicated however that there is another movement which manifests in the phenomena of the precession of the equinoxes—the movement of the point of sunrise at the spring equinox through the zodiac, once in 25,920 years. This is also the equivalent of a certain motion in human beings. What can we find within us that corresponds to it? You may be able to come to a conclusion on this point from what I have said above. We have to find a motion equivalent to the relation of the sun to the fixed stars, for the point of sunrise progresses through the complete zodiac—or fixed stars—once in 25,920 years. The equivalent in us is to be found in a relation between the forces of inner movement and the forces of form; but one which must be of long duration. The forces of inner movement in us must change in some way, so as to alter their position in relation to our external periphery.

You will remember what I said about something that has been observable since the period of ancient Greece. I said that the Greeks used the same word for 'yellow' and 'green', that they really did not see blue in the same way as we do, but actually, as reported by Roman writers, recognized and used four colours only in their art, namely, yellow, red, black and white. They saw these four living colours. To them the sky was not blue as we see it; it appeared to them as a kind of darkness. Now this is an assertion that can be made in all certainty, and spiritual science confirms it. This change in the human being has taken place since the time of ancient Greece. When you ponder the fact that the constitution of the human eye has undergone such a degree of modification since the period of ancient Greece, you can then also conceive of other alterations in the human organism, taking place at our external periphery and occupying still longer periods of time for their accomplishment. Such alterations at our periphery must of necessity bear a relation to the forces of inner movement, for, of course, they cannot be produced by the digestion or the organs. These external changes correspond, as a matter of fact, to the course of the vernal equinox in the zodiac, to a period, that is, of 25,920 years. During this period the human race undergoes complete change. We must not make the mistake of thinking that humanity was the same 25,920 years ago as it is now. Consideration of the circumstances connected with physical existence makes it absurd to use the figures given us by modern geology for the purpose of following human evolution, for we can comprise this only in the period of 25,920 years, and part of that is still in the future. When the vernal equinox has returned to the same place once more, the alterations that will have taken place in the whole human race are such that the human form will be quite dissimilar to what it is now. I have already told you something derived from other sources of cognition about the future of the human race and about its age. And here we see how the consideration of physical conditions compels a recognition of the same knowledge.

From all this you can see that what we call the 'movements of the heavenly bodies' are not quite as simple as present day astronomy would have us believe, but that we enter here into extremely complicated conditions—conditions that can be studied from a perspective which relates man to the macrocosm. I have already been able to point out to you certain details of the motions of the heavenly bodies, and we shall in course of time learn more and more about them from other sources. You will already be able to see one thing—that man is not wholly dependent upon the macrocosm. With what lies deep down in the subconscious, with the processes of metabolism and assimilation, he is still in a certain way—but *only* in a certain way—bound to the earth's daily rotation on its axis. Nevertheless, he can lift himself out of this connection. How is this? It is possible because man as he now is, built up in accordance with the forces of the periphery and of inner movement, with the forces too of the organs and of the metabolic system, is complete and finished in his dependence on external forces; and is thus able, with his complete and finished organization, to sever himself from this connection. In the same sense that we have in waking and sleeping a copy of day and night, having thus in ourselves the inner rhythm of day and night, but not needing to make this inner rhythm *correspond* with the outer rhythm of day and night (i.e. we need not sleep at night, nor wake during the day), so we can also sever our connection with the macrocosm in other parts of our existence. Upon this is founded the possibility of human *free will*. It is not man's *present* development that is dependent upon the macrocosm, but his *past* development. Man's present experiences are fundamentally a picture or copy of his past adaptation to the macrocosm, and in this sense we live in the pictures of our past. Within these we are enabled to evolve our freedom, and from them we receive our moral laws, which are independent of natural necessity. It is when we understand clearly how man and macrocosm are related to each other that we recognize the possibility of our free will.

Finally we must think over the following. It is clear that our metabolic forces still retain a certain connection with the rhythm of our daily life. The forces of form have solidified. Now consider the *animal* instead of man. Here we shall find a much more complete dependence upon the macrocosm. Man has grown out of or beyond this dependence. Ancient wisdom therefore spoke of the *zodiac* or 'Animal Circle', not of the 'Man Circle', as corresponding to formative forces. These forces manifest themselves in the animal kingdom in a great variety of forms, while in man they manifest essentially in *one* form encompassing the whole human race; but they are the forces of the animal kingdom, and as we evolve beyond them and become man, we must go out *beyond* the zodiac. Beyond the zodiac lies that upon which we, as human beings, are dependent in a higher sense than we are upon all that exists within the zodiac, that is, within the circle of the fixed stars. Beyond the zodiac is that which corresponds to our ego.

With the astral body—which the animal also possesses—we are fettered to a dependence upon the macrocosm, and the building up of the astral vehicle takes place in accordance with the will of the stars. But with our 'I' or ego we transcend this zodiac.

Here we have the principle upon which we have gained our freedom. Within the zodiac we cannot sin, any more than can the animals; we begin to sin as soon as we carry our actions beyond the zodiac. This happens when we do things that make us free from our connection with universal formative forces, when we enter into relationship with regions exterior to the zodiac or region of fixed stars. And this is the essential content of the human ego.

You see, we may measure the universe in so far as it appears to us a visible and temporal thing, we may measure its full extent through space to the outermost fixed stars, and all that takes place by way of movement in time in this starry heaven, and we may consider all this in its relation to man; but in man something is being fulfilled that occurs *outside* this space and *outside* this time, outside all that takes place in the astral. There beyond is no 'natural necessity', but only what is intimately connected with our *moral* nature and moral actions. *Within* the zodiac we are unable to evolve our moral nature; but in so far as we evolve it, we record it into the macrocosm beyond the zodiac. All that we do remains and works in the world. The processes taking place within us, from the forces forming us to the forces of metabolism, are the result of the past. But the past does not prejudge the whole of the future, it has no power over that future which proceeds *from man himself in his moral actions*.

I can only lead you forward in this study step by step. Keep well in mind what I have said today, and in my next lecture we will examine the matter from yet another point of view.

Lecture 7

The previous lectures described a path which, if followed in the right way, leads to an overall view of the universe and its organization. As you have seen, this path compels a continuous search for the harmony existing between the processes taking place within us and the processes observed in the wider universe. Tomorrow and the day after I shall have to treat our subject in such a way that the friends who have come to attend the General Meeting may be able to receive something from the two lectures at which they are present. Tomorrow I shall go over again some of what has been said in order then to connect with it something fresh.

If you read my *Occult Science—an Outline*, you will see that its description of the evolution of the known universe continually strives to relate that evolution to the evolution of man himself. Beginning with the Saturn period which was followed by the Sun and Moon periods preceding the Earth period, you will remember that the Saturn period was characterized by the laying of the first foundations of the human senses. And along this line of thought the book proceeds. Everywhere universal conditions are considered in a way that at the same time also describes the evolution of man. In short, the human being is not considered as standing in the universe in the way modern science sees him—the external universe on the one hand, and man on the other, as two entities that do not rightly belong to each other. Here, on the contrary, the two are regarded as closely interconnected, and the evolution of both is followed together. This conception must, of necessity, be applied also to the *present* attributes, forces and motions of the universe.

We cannot consider first the universe abstractly in its purely spatial aspect, as is done in the Galileo-Copernican system, and then man as existing beside it; we must allow both to merge into one another in our study.

This is only possible when we have acquired an understanding of man himself. I have already shown you how little modern science is able to explain man truly. What does science do, for instance, in that sphere where it seems greatest, judging by modern methods of thought? It states in a grand manner that man has evolved physically from other lower forms. It then shows how, during the embryonic period, the human being passes again rapidly through these forms, in recapitulation. This means that man is regarded as the highest of the animals. Science contemplates the animal kingdom and then creates man as a composite of all that is found there; in other words, it examines everything non-human, and then sees how it becomes man. Natural science does not feel called upon to study man as man, and consequently any real understanding of his nature is out of the question.

In fact, people who claim to be experts in this domain of nature nowadays really ought to examine Goethe's investigations in natural science, particularly his theory of colours. He uses a very different method of investigation from the one we are used to today. At the very outset he mentions subjective, and physiological colours; and actual phenomena, what the living human eye experiences in connection with its environment, are then carefully investigated. It is shown, for example, how these experiences or impressions do not merely last as long as the eye is exposed to its surroundings, but that an after-effect remains. You all know a very simple phenomenon connected with this. You gaze at a red surface, and then quickly turning to a white surface you will see a green after-colour. This shows that the eye is, in a certain sense, still under the influence of the original impression. There is no need, here, to examine why the second colour seen should be green, we will only keep in mind the more general fact that the eye responds to its experience with a slowly fading after-effect.

We have to do here with an experience on the periphery of the human body, for the eye is on the periphery. When we contemplate this experience, we find that for a certain limited time the eye retains the after-effect of the impression; after that the experience ceases, and the eye can then expose itself to new impressions without interference from the last one.

Let us now consider quite objectively a phenomenon connected not with any single localized organ of the human organism, but with the whole human being. Provided our observations are unprejudiced, we cannot fail to recognize that this experience, which the whole human being has, is related to the experience localized in the eye. We expose ourselves to an impression, to an experience, with our whole being. In so doing, we absorb this experience just as the eye absorbs the impression of the colour to which it is exposed; and we find that after the lapse of months, or even years, the after-effect comes forth in the form of a thought-picture. The whole phenomenon is somewhat different, but you will not fail to recognize the relation of this memory picture to that after-picture of an experience which the eye retains for a short, limited time.

This is the kind of question that we must properly ask—for we can only gain some knowledge of the world when we learn to ask questions in the right way. Let us therefore ask ourselves: What is the connection between these two phenomena—between the after-picture of the eye and the memory picture that rises up within us in relation to a certain experience? As soon as we put our question in this form and require a definite answer, we realize that the whole method of modern scientific thought completely fails to supply the answer; and it fails because of its ignorance of one great fact—the fact of the universal significance of *metamorphosis*. This metamorphosis is something that is not completed in us within the limits of one life, but only plays itself out in consecutive lives on earth.

You will remember that in order to gain a true insight into the nature of man, we distinguished three parts: head, rhythmic system and limbs. We may, for the present purpose, consider the last two as one, and we then have the head-organization on the one hand and all that makes up the remaining parts on the other. As we try to comprehend this head-organization, we must be able to understand how it is related to man's whole evolution. The head is a later metamorphosis, a transformation, of the rest of man, *considered in terms of its forces*. Were you to imagine yourself without your head—and of course also without whatever is present in the rest of the organism but really belongs to the head—you would, in the first place, think of the remaining portion of your organism in terms of the substances composing it. But here we are not concerned with substance; it is the *inter-relation of the forces* at work in this substance which undergoes a complete transformation in the period between death and a new birth and becomes our head-organization in the next incarnation. In other words, what you now include in the lower part (the rhythmic system and the limbs) is an earlier stage of what is going to metamorphose into head-organization. But if you wish to understand how this metamorphosis proceeds, you will have to consider the following.

Take any one organ—liver or kidney—of what we can call your 'lower man', and compare it with your head-organization. You will at once become aware of a fundamental, essential difference; namely, that all the activities of the lower parts of the body as distinct from the upper or head, are directed *inwards*, as instanced by the kidneys, whose whole activity is exercised within the body's interior. The activity of the kidneys is an activity of secretion. In comparing this organ with a characteristic organ of the head—the eye, for instance—you find the construction of the latter to be the exact opposite. It is directed entirely *outwards*, and the results of the changing impressions are transmitted inwards to the power of reason, to the head. In any particular organ of the head you have the polar opposite of an organ belonging to the other part of the body. We might depict this fact diagrammatically.

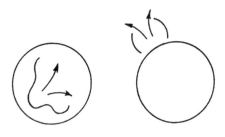

Take the drawing on the left as the first metamorphosis, and the drawing on the right as the second; then you will have to imagine the first as the first life, and the second as the second life, and between the two is the life between death and a new birth. We have first an inner organ which is directed inward. But through the transformation taking place between death and rebirth, the whole position and direction of this organ is entirely reversed—it now opens outwards. So that an organ which develops its activity inwardly in one incarnation develops it outwardly in the succeeding life. You can now imagine that something has happened between the two incarnations that may be compared with putting on a glove, taking it off and turning it inside out. Upon wearing the glove again, the surface which was previously turned inward comes outside, and vice versa. Thus it must be noted that this metamorphosis does not merely transform the organs, but turns them inside out; inner becomes outer. We can now say that the organs of the body (taking 'body' as the opposite to 'head') have been transformed. So that one or other of our abdominal organs, for instance, has now become our eyes in this incarnation. It has been reversed in its active forces, has become an eye, and has attained the capacity to generate after-effects from the external impressions it receives. Now where does this capacity originate?

Let us consider the eye and its task in life in an unbiased way. These after-effects only prove to us that the eye is a living thing. They prove that the eye retains impressions for a little while; and why? I will use as a simile something simpler. Suppose you touch silk; your organ of touch retains an after-effect of the smoothness of silk. If later on you again touch silk, you recognize it from the first impression you retained. It is the same with the eye. *The after-effect is somehow connected with recognition.* The inner activity which produces this after-effect has something to do with recognition. But an outer object we recognize remains outside us. If I see any one of you now, and tomorrow meet you again and recognize you, you will be physically present before me.

Now compare this with the inner organ of which the eye is a transformation in respect to its activity and forces. In this organ must reside something which in a certain sense corresponds to the eye's capacity for retaining pictures of impressions, something akin to the inner life of the eye; but it must be directed inward. And this must also have some connection with recognition. But to recognize an experience means to remember it. So when we look for the fundamental metamorphosis of the eye's activity in a former life, we must enquire into the activity of that organ which induces memory.

It is impossible to explain these things in simple language such as people often prefer nowadays, but we can direct our thoughts along a certain line which, if pursued, will lead us to see that all our sense-organs which are directed outward correspond to inner organs, and that these latter are also the organs of memory. With the eye we *see* what recurs as an impression from the outer world, while with those organs *within* the human body which correspond to what the eye metamorphosed from we remember the pictures transmitted through the eye. We *hear* sound with the ear, and with the inner organ corresponding to the ear we *remember* that sound. Thus the whole of us becomes, as we direct or open our organs inward, an *organ of memory*. We encounter the outer world, taking it into ourselves in the form of impressions. Materialistic science claims that we receive an impression through the eye which is transmitted to the optic nerve, and then apparently ceases; as regards the process of cognition, the whole remaining organism is thought to be as important as the fifth wheel of a waggon! But this is far from the truth. All that we perceive passes over into the rest of the organism. The nerves have no direct relation with memory. On the contrary the entire human body, the whole of us, becomes a memory instrument, only specialized in terms of particular organs. Materialism is experiencing a tragic paradox—it fails to comprehend matter, because it sticks fast to its abstractions! It becomes more and more abstract, the spiritual is more and more filtered out; therefore it cannot penetrate to the essence of material phenomena, for it does not recognize the spiritual within the material. For instance, materialism does not realize that our internal organs have very much more to do with our memory than has the brain, which merely prepares the idea or images so that they can be absorbed by the other organs of the whole body. In this connection our science perpetuates a one-sided asceticism, unwilling to understand the spirituality of the material world, and desiring to overcome it. Our science has learnt sufficient asceticism to deprive itself of the capacity for understanding the world, when it claims that the eyes and other sense-organs receive their various impressions, pass them on to the nervous system and then to something else, which remains undefined. But this undefined 'something' is the entire remaining organism! Here it is that memories originate through the recollective response of the organs.

This was very well known in the days when no spurious asceticism burdened human perception. Thus we find that the ancients, when speaking of 'hypochondria' for example, did not speak of it in the same way as people generally do nowadays, and even the psycho-analyst when he maintains that hypochondria is merely mental, is something rooted in the soul. No, hypochondria means a hardening of the abdominal and lower region. The ancients knew well enough that this hardening of the abdominal system results in what we call hypochondria, and the English language, which gives evidence of a less advanced stage than other European tongues, still contains a remnant of memory of this correspondence between the material and the spiritual. I can, at the moment, only remind you of one instance of this. In English, depression is called 'spleen'. The word is the same as the name of the physical organ that has very much to do with this depression. For this condition of soul cannot be explained by examining the nervous system; instead, it is rooted in the spleen. We might find a good many such correspondences, for the genius of language has preserved much; and even if words have been somewhat transformed as they came to be applied to the soul, yet they reflect the real insight man once possessed in ancient times and that stood him in good stead.

To repeat—as entire human being you observe the surrounding world, and this world reacts upon your organs, which adapt themselves to these experiences according to their nature. In a medical school, when anatomy is being studied, the liver is just called liver, be it the liver of a man of 50 or of 25, of a musician or of one who understands as much of music as a cow does of Sunday after feasting on grass for a week! It is simply liver. The fact is that a great difference exists between the liver of a musician and that of a non-musician, for the liver is very closely connected with all that may be summed up as the musical conceptions that live and resound in man. It is of no use to look at the liver with the eye of an ascetic and see it as an inferior organ; for that apparently humble organ is the seat of all that lives in and expresses itself through the beautiful sequence of melody; it is closely concerned, for example, with the act of listening to a symphony. We must clearly understand that the liver also possesses an etheric organ; it is this latter which, in the first place, has to do with music. But the outer physical liver is, in a certain sense, an externalization of the etheric liver, and its form is like the form of the latter. In this way you see, you prepare your organs; and if it depended entirely upon yourself, the instruments of your senses would, in the next incarnation, be a replica of the experiences you had accrued in the world in the present incarnation. But this is true only to a certain extent, for in the interval between death and a new birth beings of the higher hierarchies come to our aid, and they do not always decide that we should continue to carry the destiny of injuries produced upon our organs by lack of knowledge or of self-control. We receive help between death and re-birth, and therefore this part of our constitution is not dependent upon ourselves alone.

From all this you will see that a relation really exists between the head-organization and the rest of the body with its organs. The body becomes head, and we lose the head at death in so far as its formative forces are concerned. Therefore it is so essentially bony in its structure and is preserved longer on earth than the rest of the organism, which fact is only the outer sign that it plays no further part in our following reincarnation, and in all that we have to experience between death and rebirth. Ancient atavistic wisdom perceived these things plainly, and especially when that great relation between man and macrocosm was investigated, which we find expressed in ancient descriptions of the movements of heavenly bodies. The genius of language has also preserved a great deal here. As I pointed out yesterday, physically we adhere internally to the day-cycle. We demand breakfast *every day*, and not only on Sunday. Breakfast, dinner and supper are required every day, and not only breakfast on Sunday, dinner on Wednesday and supper on Saturday. We are bound to the 24-hour cycle in respect to our metabolism—or the transmutation of matter from the outer world. This day-cycle within us corresponds to the daily motion of the earth upon its axis. These things were closely perceived by ancient wisdom. People did not feel they were separate from the earth, for they knew that they conformed to its motions; they also knew the nature of what they conformed to. Those who have an understanding for ancient works of art—though the examples still preserved today offer but little opportunity for studying these things—will be aware of a living sense, on the part of the ancients, of the connection of man the microcosm with the macrocosm. This is clear from the position certain figures take up in their pictures, and the position that certain others are beginning to assume etc., which continually reflect cosmic movements.

But we shall find something of even greater significance if we examine something else. Almost all the peoples of this earth make a clear distinction between the week and the day. On the one hand stands the cycle of the transmutation of substances—or metabolism—which expresses itself in the taking of meals at regular intervals. But human beings have never reckoned according to this cycle alone, adding to the day-cycle a week-cycle. Human beings first distinguished the rising and setting of the sun, which corresponds to a *day*; then they repeated it cyclically in Sunday, Monday, Tuesday, Wednesday, Thursday, Friday and Saturday, a cycle seven times that of the other, returning once again to Sunday. We experience this in the contrast between *day* and *week*. But man wished to express a great deal more by this contrast. He wished first to show the connection of the daily cycle with the motion of the sun.

Thus there is a cycle seven times as great as the daily rhythm, which, whilst returning again to the sun, includes all the planets—Sun, Moon, Mercury, Venus, Mars, Jupiter and

Saturn. This is the weekly cycle. This was intended to signify that, having one cycle corresponding to a day, and one seven times greater that included the planets, not only does the earth revolve upon its axis (or the sun go round), but the *whole system* is also in movement. This movement can be seen in various other examples. If you take the cycle of the year, then you have in the year, as you know, 52 weeks, so that seven weeks is, numerically, roughly a seventh part of the year. This means, taking the period from the beginning to the end of the year in terms of its weeks, that we must imagine the weekly cycle taking place at a different speed from what occurs through the daily cycle.

And where are we to look for the origin of the feeling which impels us to reckon, now with the day-cycle, and now with the week-cycle? It arises from the sensation within us of the contrast between human head-development and that of the rest of the organism. We see the human head-organization represented by a process to which I have already drawn your attention—the formation, within about a year's cycle, of the first teeth.

If you consider the first and second dentition you will see that the second takes place after a cycle that is seven times as long as the cycle of the first dentition. We may say that the one-year cycle of the first dentition relates to the developmental cycle active until the second dentition in the same way as the day relates to the week. The ancients felt this to be true, because they rightly understood another thing. They understood that the first dentition was primarily the result of heredity. You only need look at the embryo to realize that its development proceeds out of the head-organization, and the remainder of the organism is added later. You will then understand that the ancients were quite correct when they saw a connection of the formation of the *first teeth* with the *head* and of the *second teeth* with the *whole human organism*. And today we must arrive at the same result if we consider these phenomena objectively. The first teeth are connected with the forces of the human head, the second with the forces that work from the rest of the organism and penetrate into the head.

Through looking at the matter in this way, we have arrived at an important difference between the head and the rest of the human body. The difference is one which can, in the first place, be considered as connected with *time*, for that which takes place in the human head has a seven times greater rapidity than that which takes place in the rest of the human organism. Let us translate this into rational language. Let us say that today you have eaten your usual number of meals in the proper sequence. Your *organism* demands a repetition of them tomorrow. Not so the *head*. This acts according to another measure of time; it must wait *seven days* before the food taken into the rest of the organism has proceeded far enough to enable the head to assimilate it. Supposing this to be Sunday, your head would have to wait until next Sunday before it would be in a position to benefit from the fruit of today's Sunday dinner. In the head-organization, a repetition takes place after a period of seven days of what has been accomplished seven days before in the organism. All this the ancients knew intuitively and expressed by saying: a week is necessary to transmute what is physical and bodily into soul and spirit.

You will now see that the metamorphosis occurring between death and rebirth also brings about a repetition in 'simple' time in the succeeding incarnation of what requires a seven times longer period to be accomplished. We are thus concerned with a metamorphosis which is *spatial* through the fact that our remaining organism—our body—is not merely transformed, but turned inside out, and is at the same time *temporal*, in that our head-organization works seven times more quickly.

It will be clear to you now that this human organization is

not, after all, quite so simple as our modern, comfort-loving science would like to believe. We must make up our mind to regard man's organization as much more complicated; for if we do not understand this rightly, we are also prevented from realizing the cosmic movements in which we take part. The descriptions of the universe circulated in modern times are mere abstractions, for they do not rest on a knowledge of man.

The new perspective needed, above all by astronomy, is one requiring the re-inclusion of *man* in the scheme of things, when cosmic movements are being studied. Such studies will then naturally be somewhat more difficult.

Goethe had an intuitive sense of the metamorphosis of the skull from the vertebrae, when, in a Jewish burial ground in Venice, he found a sheep's skull which had fallen apart into its various small sections; these enabled him to study the transformation of the vertebrae, and he then pursued his discovery in detail. Modern science has also touched upon this line of research. You will find some interesting observations relating to the matter, and some hypotheses derived from it, by the comparative anatomist Karl Gegenbaur; but in reality Gegenbaur created obstacles to Goethean intuitional research, for he failed to find sufficient reason to declare himself in favour of the parallel between the vertebrae and the single sections of the skull. Why did he fail to do so? Because so long as people think only of a *metamorphosis* and disregard the *inside out inversion*, they will gain only an approximate idea of the similarity of the two kinds of bones. For in reality the bones of the skull result from those forces which act upon man between death and rebirth, and they are therefore bound to be essentially different in appearance from merely transformed bone. They are turned inside out; it is this reversal which is the important point.

Imagine we have here (diagram) the upper or head realm. All influences or impressions proceed inward from without.

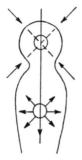

Here below would be the rest of the human body. Here everything works from within outwards, but so as to remain within the organism. Let me put it in another way. With his head man stands in relation to his outer environment, while with his lower organism he is related to the processes taking place within himself. The abstract mystic says: 'Look within to find the reality of the outer world.' But this is merely abstract thought. The reality of the outer world is *not* found through inner contemplation of all that acts upon us from outside; we must go deeper and consider the two different realms within us, and allow the world to take form in quite a different part of our being. That is why abstract mysticism yields so little fruit, and why it is necessary to think here too of an inner process, not merely of an abstract transformation of what we find outside us.

I do not expect any of you to allow your dinner to stand before you untouched, and appease your hunger merely through its attractive appearance! Life could not be sustained in this way. No! We must induce that process which runs its course in the 24-hour cycle, and which, if we consider the whole man, including the upper or head-organization, only finishes its course after seven days. But that which is assimilated spiritually—for it has really to be assimilated and not merely contemplated!—also requires for this process a period seven times as long. Therefore it becomes necessary first intellectually to assimilate all we absorb. But to see it reborn again within us, we must wait seven years. Only then has it developed into what it was intended to be. That is why after the founding of the Anthroposophical Society in 1901 we had to wait patiently, seven, and then even fourteen years for the result!*

---

*The formal institution of the Anthroposophical Society took place in February 1913.

Lecture 8

I would like to bring forward again, in a rather different form, a few remarks made in the course of our studies. You know that the fact of the intimate relation between man and the universe was much more easily accessible to the perception and knowledge of the ancients than is the case in our present day. If we were to go back to the period of Egypto-Chaldean culture, we should find that man did not look upon himself as a separate being who simply walks about on the earth, but as a being belonging to the whole universe. He knew of course to begin with that in a certain sense he was dependent upon the earth. That can easily be observed; even our own materialistic age admits that, as far as our physical metabolism is concerned, we depend upon the earth's products, which we assimilate. But in those ancient times, by means of course of atavistic perception, man knew himself to be dependent, also in his *soul*, on the one hand on the elements of fire, water and air, and on the other hand on the movements of the planets. These he related to his soul-nature in the same way as he related the products of the earth to his physical metabolism. And the part of the universe that is outside or beyond the planetary system, all that is in the starry heavens—this he connected with his *spirit*.

Thus in those past ages, when there was no thought of materialism, man knew himself to be living in the bosom of the universe. You may now say: Yes, but how is it that people of those times made such big mistakes about the movements of the heavenly bodies, while today, in this materialistic age, we have made such magnificent progress in relation to the real truth of these movements? Well, we have been speaking of these things for some time and we have seen that people's belief about the movements of the heavenly bodies, based on what science asserts, derives from certain prejudices. Upon this subject I shall have more to say tomorrow, but for the moment we may remind ourselves that modern man has entirely lost consciousness of the fact that what belongs to our whole constitution can no more be discovered in the physical world than in the visible stellar world. For it is absolutely impossible to gain a true perception even of the visible starry heavens unless we combine the super-physical with outer physical life—that super-physical part of our life through which we pass between death and re-birth. Yesterday we drew attention to the metamorphosis that takes place in us through this alternation between earthly and super-earthly life and showed how the organs which we consider as belonging to our lower realm (and of which we said yesterday that they open inwards), transform themselves—as regards their *forces*, though obviously not in their substance—during the period between death and a new birth, and become what is considered to be the more noble head-organism. This latter is in reality nothing more than the metamorphosis—as regards the structure of its forces—of our so-called 'lower' region from our last earth-life.

If we really think this matter over, we can see—in spirit— how between death and rebirth, man has a certain content within him of his experiences, as he has also here between birth and death. But the content is essentially different in each case. We may make this difference clear by saying: Between birth and death, we have space as the circumference for our experiences, and also what takes place in time. We inhabit space and time.

You know in how small a degree people really experience the processes within their inner organism. They are not conscious of them, being much more aware of what is outside them. Everything within the skin is known to man only indirectly and incompletely. The knowledge gained through anatomy and physiology is not real knowledge, for we do not thereby learn to look into our actual interior; it is an illusion to believe that we do. Spiritual science alone gradually reveals all that is within man. But what happens between death and a new birth? In a certain sense we look then *from the periphery to the centre*. And we then know just as little of the periphery as we do here of our centre or interior. During this period we have instead a direct perception of the secrets and mysteries of man himself. That which is hidden within us—within our skin—becomes observed experience for us between death and a new birth.

Now perhaps you will say that this world which we observe during the time between death and rebirth must be a very small one indeed. But spatial dimensions do not count at all. It is the fullness or poverty of the content that matters, not the size. If we combine all we observe in the mineral, plant and animal kingdoms, and add thereto the starry heavens, it would not compare in richness with the mysteries within man himself. The real process is approximately as follows. We lose the structural forces of the head when we pass over into death. They have completed their task. But then the spiritual world takes up the formative forces of the remaining (lower) organism, which from being inner experience belong now to the periphery, and transforms them in such a way that when the time is ripe the spiritual world fashions them into the human *head* in the womb of the mother.

We must be absolutely clear upon this point. The very first beginnings of the physical human being that develop within the mother are produced by the whole cosmos. Conception is merely the opportunity given for a certain cosmic activity to penetrate the human body, and what forms first in the process of human embryonic development is indeed an image of the whole cosmos. Those who wish to study the human embryo from its first stage onwards must consider it as an image of the cosmos.

These matters are almost entirely overlooked today. For of what do we generally think when we speak of the origin of a human being in the physical sense? Of heredity! We observe how the child-organism is formed within the parent-organism, and we are ignorant of how the cosmic forces which surround us are active within the parent-organism; we are ignorant of the fact that the whole macrocosm endows the human being with its forces in order to make possible the genesis of a new human being.

Of course, the great fault of the modern outlook is that we never take the macrocosm into consideration, and therefore never become conscious of the origin of the forces whose effect we observe. I must once again remind you of the following. The modern physicist or chemist says that there are molecules which are composed of atoms, that the atoms possess forces by means of which they act upon each other. Now this is a conception which simply does not accord with reality. The truth is that the minutest molecule is acted upon by the *whole starry heavens*. Suppose here is a planet, here another, here another, and so on. Then there are the fixed stars, which imbue the molecule with their forces. All these lines of force intersect each other in various ways. The planets also transmit their forces in the same way, and we come to realize that the molecule is nothing but *a focus of macrocosmic forces*. It is the ardent desire of modern science to bring microscopy far enough to enable the atoms to be seen within the molecule. This way of looking at things must cease. Instead of wishing to examine the structure of the molecule microscopically, we must turn our gaze outwards to the starry heavens, we must look at the constellations and see copper in one, tin in another! It is out there in the macrocosm that we need to behold the structure of the molecule that is only *reflected* in the molecule. Instead of passing into the infinitely small, we must turn our gaze outwards to the infinitely great, for it is there we have to look for the reality of what lives in minuscule processes.

This materialistic conception of things also affects other domains of thought. Someone who considers himself capable of giving an opinion on the progress of human knowledge may say: Nineteenth century materialism is now overcome! But it isn't! It is not overcome so long as people still think atomistically, so long as they fail to search in the wider universe for the form and configuration of the small. Neither is the materialism relating to humanity overcome, so long as we continue to ignore the connection of man the microcosm with the macrocosm.

And at this point we encounter a new—I might say a monstrous—evidence of materialism, to which I have previously drawn attention. It is in so-called theosophy that its traces are often to be found, where a tendency is present to look at things in the following way. Here we have matter; then ether, thinner than matter but otherwise similar to physical matter; then comes the astral—again thinner or finer than the etheric; and after that quite a number of other beautiful things, all thinner and thinner and thinner. Call it astral world, kama-manas, or what you will, it is not spiritual, but remains materialistic! The truth is that in order to arrive at a real understanding of the world, we must conceive of heavy, ponderable matter as ceasing at the *ether* level; for we must clearly understand that this ether is essentially a very different thing from that substance of which we speak as filling space. When speaking of this latter substance, we think of space as filled with matter. But this we cannot do when we speak of ether, for then we must conceive space as being empty of matter. When ordinary matter strikes some other object, the object is repelled or pushed away. When ether approaches an object, it attracts it and draws it into itself. The activity of ether is the exact opposite to that of matter. Ether acts as an absorbent force. Were this otherwise, you would present the same appearance back and front, for even in this diversity of the physical appearance of man we have the result on the one hand of the pressure of ponderable matter, and on the other of the absorbing action of ether. Your nose is forced outwards, as it were, from your organism through the pressure of matter, while the eye sockets are drawn inward through the action of ether. It is therefore simply a pressing and absorbing substance acting within you which differentiates the exterior appearance of your front and back. These are things which are not usually taken into consideration.

Further, when we come to speak of the astral, we must not think of three-dimensional physical matter extending in a threefold way in space, nor must we think of the absorbent ether, but of a third factor, one that forms the adjustment or connection between the other two. And should we then go on and attempt to form some approximate idea of that part of our being termed the ego—the 'I am'—we would have to include a fourth factor, which acts as mediator between, on the one hand, the absorbent-repelling action of ether and physical matter, and on the other hand, the astral substance. These are the things that must be taken into consideration.

If the ether has merely a sucking, absorbing action, you might ask, how then is it possible for us to perceive it? But this would be a misapprehension. The fact is, ether stands, figuratively speaking, in the same relation to ponderable matter—I am speaking metaphorically now—as the relation we find in another plane if we have a bottle of soda-water. We may not see the transparent water in the bottle, but the pearly bubbles we can see, although these are 'thinner' than the water. And so ether, which is an absence of physical matter and therefore its essential antithesis, can in fact be perceived.

From the foregoing you will now see that it is necessary, when speaking of the life between death and rebirth, to realize that this life is actually lived *beyond space*—beyond the space of which we are aware on the earth-plane; and we shall have to endeavour to gain a conception of this 'beyond' of space. You can best do so by trying first to imagine 'filled' space. Take for instance a table; it fills or occupies space. Then you pass from 'filled' space to 'empty' space, and perhaps you would say that you cannot go beyond this. But as I have previously pointed out to you, this would be about as sensible as to say: 'I have a full purse out of which I continue to take money till nothing is left; this "nothing" cannot be less than it is.' But it can be less if you get into debt, when you would have less than nothing in your purse! Similarly, empty space can be less than empty by being filled with ether, when it becomes a negative entity.

And what mediates between the two, what also mediates within you between forces of pressure and suction, is the astral. No relationship would exist between the front and back of a human body did not the astral activity within form the connection between the effects of suction and pressure. You will say: I do not observe this connecting element. But try to follow the digestive process and you will find the connecting link very clearly manifested. The astral is active there, and its activity is based upon the contrast between the front and back nature of the human being, even as the astral mediation between our higher (head) realm and lower (limb) realm depends upon the ego. We must therefore consider man, as he stands before us, in a quite concrete manner and make clear to ourselves that while he has existence upon this plane between birth and death he imprints his astral nature and his ego in what absorbs and what exerts pressure, but when he dies he carries his being back to what only manifests here on earth as the mediator between front and back, and between his upper and lower realms.

Now, what is this mediating or connecting link? It is what we experience within us when we feel our equilibrium. We do not jerk the head forward and backward; we stand and walk *erect*. We accommodate our posture to the demands of the laws of equilibrium. We cannot *see* this, but we experience it inwardly. When we pass through the gate of death we consciously adjust ourselves to this condition, of which here we take no heed. If we possessed eyes only, it would then be dark around us, and if we had ears only, stillness would envelop us. But we have also the *sense of balance*, and the *sense of motion*, and so we become able after all to 'experience' things after death. We take part in that which on earth is implied in the words 'balance' and 'movement'. We adapt ourselves to the movements of the external world, we find our way into them.

You see, here, in the life between birth and death, the only way we experience the activity of the earth's rotation upon its axis is in our daily metabolic process. We must take our daily meals; and this together with the succeeding digestive processes takes place within a 24-hour-cycle, uniform with one revolution of the earth. These two things belong together, the one is proof of the other. When we die, the revolution of the earth becomes something *real* to us, as real as are the visible objects here. Then we *live* in this terrestrial motion; we begin to experience this motion consciously.

There are also other motions connected with the starry heavens, all of which we experience after death. Correctly considered we do not expand into the cosmos like a jellyfish, but we take part in the life of the cosmos—and as beings taking part in cosmic life we experience at the same time the interior of the human organism. Between birth and death we say: My heart is within my breast, and in it converge the streams or motions of blood-circulation. At a certain stage of development between death and rebirth we say: In my inner being is the sun—and by this we mean the actual sun, which the physicist claims to be a ball of gas, but which is in reality something quite different. We experience the actual sun in the same manner as we experience our heart here on earth. Here the sun is visible to the eye, whereas during the time between death and rebirth the evolution of the heart on its path to the pineal gland, as it undergoes a wonderful metamorphosis, is the cause of sublime experiences. We experience the complete system of our blood-circulation—the forces at work in it, that is, not the substances as such. As existence between death and rebirth proceeds, these forces undergo transmutation, so that, when once again we come to be born on earth, they become the forces of our new nervous system. Look at the plates and illustrations scattered through modern books on anatomy or physiology and examine the circulatory system of the blood in *one* incarnation. In the *next* incarnation this becomes what lives in the nerves. We must not think of the head, breast (rhythmic) and limb systems too schematically, as separate from one another, for they interpenetrate each other. Note the wonderful structure of the human eye; there we find blood-vessels, choroid and retina (omentum). The last two are transformations of each other. What today is retina was in the last incarnation choroid, and what is choroid today will be retina in the next incarnation. Of course this must not be taken too literally, but this gives an approximate idea of things. So you will understand that we cannot gain true understanding of man if we merely study him as he appears between birth and death or even along the lines by which he develops through the forces of physical heredity. For this will, at most, only allow us insight into the circulatory system and nothing more. The nervous system of the present life is a result of a former life, and can never be understood if studied in connection with the present life alone.

Now my dear friends, I beg of you not to object to what I have explained, by saying that animals also have a nervous system although they have no former lives. Such an objection would indeed be very short-sighted; for though the forces of the human nervous system are the metamorphosis of the blood-circulation of a former life, that does not imply that the same applies in the case of animals. It would be just as logical to go to a barber and ask him to sell you a razor for the dinner-table—a razor being a knife, and knives forming part of the dinner service! Razors however do not! Nothing carries *within itself* its immediate purpose, neither does a physical organ. The human organ is entirely different from the animal organ. It depends upon the use to be made of an organ. We should not compare the human nervous system with that of an animal, but rather observe the fact that human nerves have become similar—during the course of their evolution—to animal nerves, just as the razor has a certain similarity with a table-knife. This once more shows that when people follow the ordinary materialistic line of investigation they can arrive at no true conclusion. Yet that is the path, of course, which is generally followed today.

It is this kind of method that prevents us from arriving at a conception of man as a *product of the spiritual world*. Our religious creeds, as they have gradually developed, have really been over-subservient to human egoism. It may almost be said that their one and only aim is to convince their followers of a continuation of life after death, because the egoism of humanity demands it. Yet it is equally important to prove that this life was preceded by a pre-natal life. Then people can say: 'Here upon this earth I have to be a continuation of what I was between death and my present birth. I have to continue a spiritual life here on this plane.' This is not so likely to gratify our egoism, but it is something that our civilization needs to become aware of, so that humanity can extricate itself from its anti-social instincts. Try to imagine what it will mean when we can look upon a human countenance and say: 'That is not of this world. The spiritual world has been at work upon it between the last death and this birth.' For a time will come when we shall see within the material the imprint of this spiritual work between death and rebirth. A very different kind of culture will then guide humanity, and it will bring in its train very different convictions and tendencies of thought, which will not countenance any idea of the cosmos as a vast machine set in motion by Newtonian forces of attraction between the stars. This kind of abstraction has already reached its zenith. Abstraction is deeply rooted in our ordinary conception of the planetary system, and it produces some very strange results nowadays. For example, a great deal of popular literature is permeated with glorification of an idea which originates from Einstein. This idea is said to have shaken the theory of gravity. Imagine that far away from all celestial bodies—so that any interference from a gravitational field may be excluded—there is a box. Inside it is a man who holds a stone in one hand, and some down-feathers in the other. He lets go of both and see—they begin to fall—and fall until they reach the ground in this box. Yes, says Einstein, people will no doubt say that the stone and the down both fall to the ground. But it *need* not be so; for up above a rope may be fastened (where or how I've no idea!) and by some means or other the box is drawn up. The stone and the down—owing to the absence of any celestial body—do not fall, but *remain where they are.* When the bottom of the box reaches them, it takes them up with it.

This kind of extreme abstraction can be found in the modern theory of relativity which Albert Einstein has propounded. Just think how far humanity has strayed from actuality! We can talk of relativity—well and good—but just imagine what would happen were this picture taken in earnest! A box, some inconceivable distance away from any celestial body that might attract (by gravity) the stone and the down; and inside this box a man (air is only found of course in the neighbourhood of heavenly bodies, but the man is quite happy and content; as for his stone and his down, they of course need no air!), and now the box is suspended from outside and is then lifted up!

All this is a further development of the theory of Newton who postulated a 'push' or impetus imparted to a globe at a tangent, so that centrifugal combines with centripetal force. Such things as these actually form the contents of scientific discussions today, and are considered great achievements, whereas they are nothing more than a testimony to the fact that we have arrived at the most extreme abstraction, and that materialism has produced a state of complete ignorance in humanity as to what matter really is, and caused people to live in a series of mental pictures far removed from all reality.

But, my dear friends, no consideration is given to these things nowadays, and we find our newspapers proclaiming that a new discovery has been made: the theory of gravity has been replaced by the theory of inertia. The stone and down are not attracted; they remain in their original place—perhaps only because we can manage to imagine such a thing—while the box is raised! One can truly say that so much nonsense masquerades as genius today that it becomes difficult to distinguish the one from the other. Can we wonder that people's ideas have gone haywire in many other areas of thought as well, and that this has finally resulted in what has happened in the world over the last five or six years! These are things we need to keep reminding ourselves of.

Today I needed to remind you of all this, and tomorrow I will add something further concerning the structure of the universe.

Lecture 9

The task underlying our present studies is, in the widest sense, to try to understand the universe through our interconnection and relationship with it. I am far from wishing to convey the idea to those who have had certain glimpses into the universe during the foregoing lectures that the truth of these matters can be found in any quick and easy way, such as one finds in ordinary astronomy when it tells of the celestial motions. I would, however, like the friends who have come to the General Meeting not merely to hear something that comes right in the middle of a consecutive series of lectures but, from these lectures held during the General Meeting, to take away with them a self-contained picture that can stand on its own. I will therefore continue our studies of yesterday in a particular way, and give no more than an indication of how the conception of the nature of man leads to the conception of the universe, its nature and its movements. Of course, this subject is so vast that it is impossible to exhaust it for the friends who are now present. It will be continued later. For the benefit of those here for the first time tonight, I should like to put before them at any rate a few of the salient features of what has arisen in previous lectures.

From other lectures you all know of the relationship in human life between waking and sleeping. You know that in the abstract the relation is something like this: in the waking condition, physical, etheric and astral bodies, together with the ego-being, are in a certain inner connection whereas during sleep the physical and etheric bodies are united, but the astral body and ego are separated from them—at any rate in comparison with the waking state. This, as you know however, is merely an abstract observation, for I have often emphasized that everything belonging to our limb-nature— which, continued into our inner organization, is also the real bearer of metabolism—all this part of us, connected as it is at the same time with the human will, is really in a perpetual state of sleep. We must be absolutely clear that, while we are awake, this state of sleep continues as far as our inner organism is concerned. We can therefore say that our 'limb-being' as bearer of our 'will-being' is in a permanent state of sleep. Our circulation or 'rhythmic-being', which may be described as mediating between the head-organization and our limb-being (the latter extending into our interior in metabolism), is in a continuous dream state. This rhythmic system is at the same time the outer instrument for our world of feeling. The world of feeling is rooted wholly within our rhythmic organization. And while our metabolic system, together with its outward extension, the limbs, is the vehicle of the will, the rhythmic system is the vehicle of our feeling life, and is related to our consciousness in the same way as our dream state to our waking life. Between waking and falling asleep, we are only really *awake* in our life of ideation and thought.

Thus man, in his life between birth and death, is in an intermittent waking state in respect to his life of thought, in a dream state regarding his emotions and feelings, of which the rhythmic system is the vehicle; and in a state of continuous sleep as regards his limbs and metabolic system. We must realize at this point that really to understand human nature it is necessary to fix our attention upon the fact that our limb-nature extends inwards. All the processes that are ultimately connected with the abdominal region, everything connected with assimilation, digestion, as also with the secretion of milk in females, and so forth, all these processes are a continuation of limb nature, but directed inwards. So that in speaking of the will-nature or metabolic-nature, we do not mean only the outer limbs, but the continuation inwards too of this limb activity. In relation to all this, intimately connected as it is with our will-nature, we are continuously asleep. This complicates the abstract idea we gain in the first place of the departure of the ego and astral body when we fall asleep; and it also necessitates clarification of another important fact.

When the materialistic physiologist of today speaks of the will, saying for instance that it manifests in the movement of the limbs, he has in mind that some kind of telephonic signal is sent from the central organ, the brain, proceeds through the so-called motor-nerves, and thus moves the right leg, for instance. This however is quite unproven—in fact, a quite erroneous hypothesis! For spiritual observation shows the following: when someone's will allows him to raise his right leg, his ego being exerts a direct influence upon that limb, so that it is really raised by the ego being itself; but the process takes place in a state like that of sleep. Consciousness knows nothing of it. The nerve merely informs us that we *have* a limb, it tells us of the presence of such a limb. This nerve as such has no part in the activity of the ego upon that limb. A direct correspondence exists between the limb and the will, which latter is associated in man with the ego, and in the animal with the astral body. All that physiology has to say, for instance, about the speed of transmission of the so-called will needs to be revised; for this relates, rather, to the velocity of transmission of the *perception* of that particular limb. Naturally anyone versed in modern physiology can challenge this assertion in a dozen ways. I am well acquainted with these objections. But we have to try to use a really logical thought process in this matter, and we shall find that what I say here corresponds with actual, observable facts, while what is said in physiological text-books does not.

Sometimes indeed these things are so obvious as to be evident to all. Thus at a meeting of scientists in Italy—I think it was in the 80s of the last century—a most interesting discussion took place about the contradictions which came to light between the usual theory of the motor nerves and the actual movement of a limb. But since modern physiology takes little account of the *spiritual* aspect of things, even during a discussion such as this, the only conclusions drawn were that contradictions existed in the hypothetical explanation of a certain fact. It would be extremely interesting if our learned friends, and there are such among us, were to investigate and test the physiological and biological literature of the last 40 years. They would make extremely interesting discoveries, were they to take up these subjects. They would find facts everywhere which merely need handling in the proper way to confirm the findings of spiritual science. It would form one of the most interesting tasks of the research institutes we need to start up, if the following were done. First we should carefully study international literature on the subject. We must take the *international* literature, for in English, and particularly in American literature, most interesting facts have been discovered, although these investigators do not know what to make of them. If you look into these discovered facts and substantiate them, there is but one step more needed in the sequence of investigation—given the right kind of vision in response to which the thing will, as it were, come out and show itself—and magnificent results would be arrived at. Once we have reached the stage of establishing such an institute, furnished with adequate apparatus and the necessary material, the facts will be found all around us, *waiting* as it were. People still fail to notice the urgent need for an institute such as I have in mind; series of tests and experiments are always discontinued just at the most critical moments, simply because people are ignorant of the ultimate direction of such experiments. Really important foundations would be laid by such an institute, foundations for practical work. People do not dream at the present time of the technology that would result if these things were actually done, first as experiments and then building further from there. It is only the possibility of practical work that is lacking.

This is only by the way. To return to our subject. We have to do with a part of the human being which sleeps even while he is awake. I now wish to bring to your notice a fact which has played an important part in all older conceptions and knowledge about the universe. I refer to the idea that the moon rules the lower limbs, while the region of the larynx, which we may consider as the meeting-point of the higher limbs, is associated with Mars. People of today who are deeply embedded in a modern outlook cannot of course make any-thing of such ideas; and the nonsense which hazy mystics and theosophists of today say or write about these things should not be awarded any special value, for these facts lie far deeper than, for instance, the repeated statements of materialistic theosophy that we have first coarse physical matter, and then other rather 'finer', then the astral still 'finer' and so forth. Those and similar things that pass for theosophy are in reality no spiritual teaching at all, but a spiritual *untruth*, for they are nothing more than a perpetuation of materialism.

But things that have come down to us as remnants of ancient wisdom have power to lead us to a state of real veneration and deep humility for that ancient knowledge of man, as soon as we begin to understand its meaning. Such ancient wisdom persisted not only long into the Middle Ages, but even up to the eighteenth century (where remnants of it may be found in the literature of the period), and perhaps into the nineteenth century, though here it has become mere pale reflection, so to speak, and is no longer the direct result of an original primordial consciousness. And when these things are found introduced into quite modern literature, then they are still more certain to be pale reflections. Up to the earlier part of the eighteenth century, however, we can still find traces of a certain consciousness of these things, and here again an association was construed between the nature of the moon and this region of the human organism.

What I have just said—that, in our will-metabolic nature we are in a constant state of sleep—is most forcibly expressed in the lower limbs. In other words, through the metamorphosis which the arms and hands have undergone, man wrests from unconsciousness what is really the sleep-nature of our limb system. If to some degree we sharpen our sensitivity for these things, we shall perceive what a really remarkable difference exists between the movement of a *leg* and the movement of an *arm*. The movements of the arms are free, and in a sense follow the feelings. The movement of the legs is not as free—I mean the laws underlying their movements. This, of course, is something which is not always noticed, nor sufficiently appreciated, as exemplified by the fact that the greater portion of the public attending our eurythmy performances are merely passive observers, and fail to notice that the leg movements are less articulated and the movements of the arms and hands more so. The reason for this is that, to understand the movements of the arms, a certain co-operation of the soul on the part of the observer is necessary. In our cinema age, people do not want to give this co-operation. If you watch the movements of a dance where only the legs are dancing, and the movement of the arms is fairly arbitrary, there is little need either to think or feel in union with the dancer. I mention this only in passing.

As we have seen, the most intensely unconscious process is at work in the movements of the lower limbs. There we are, in a sense, fast asleep. People entirely fail to notice how the will works into the legs or into the abdominal region, owing to this state of sleep. Our own nature only conveys a reflection of this process to us. Of course we observe the movements of our legs, but this observation does not make us conscious of the processes taking place in the nervous system as the will acts upon it; only the *reflection* of this becomes manifest to us. The nature of our lower being turns one side away, as it were, and only the other side is turned towards us. It is exactly the same with the moon. She revolves round the earth, and is altogether a most courteous lady, who never turns her back upon us, but shows us always the same aspect. She does not show us first one side, and then the other, on her journey round the earth. Nobody has ever seen her back. Because of this we never receive anything from the moon which may be termed her own, but always a reflected light. In this fact we have an absolute inner parallel between moon-nature and the whole inner being of man. As we look up to the moon, we understand her only as regards her external, formal side, but we should try to feel her inner relationship with the lower physical organization of man. The deeper we go into these matters, the more we find this to hold good. It was the simple, instinctive observations of the ancients which enabled them to realize these inner relations between human nature and the celestial bodies.

Now let us take the other fact—that the arms, in their connection with the upper portion of the middle or rhythmic system, in a sense come awake in man; the movements of the arms can be taken as equivalent at least to the dream-state. We feel that the activity of the arms is related in a much nearer sense to human consciousness than is the activity of the lower limbs. Hence we find that a person swayed by feelings generally accompanies his speech, which is in close relation to the middle, rhythmic system, with a gesture of the arms, by way of emphasis or as a help in explaining his meaning. Speech is closely related to the upper part of our rhythmic-being. I do not suppose there are many speakers who use movements of the legs as a help for speech, or many audiences who would consider such movements attractive!

So if we have the right feeling for this necessity or tendency in man's nature, we can also feel the real relationship between the hands and arms, which belong to the upper portion of the limb-system, and the middle-being or *rhythmic*-being, with its spiritual counterpart in feeling. Quite naturally we try to support our speech, which is often in danger of becoming too abstract, by gestures of our arms and hands. We endeavour to project our emotional nature into our speech. Today, in many circles—I will not name them—it is considered a sign of intellectual clarity to abstain as much as possible from using gesture in speech. We may, however, look at the matter from another standpoint and say: If a person acquires the habit of putting his hands in his trouser pockets while speaking, it may not only mark him as a man of linguistic ability, but also perhaps as being somewhat blasé. That is another aspect of the matter. I am not speaking in favour of either of these points of view, but you will see how the nature of the arms clearly indicates their connection not only with the metabolic limb system, but also with the middle, the rhythmic or circulation system. This was understood and felt by the ancients when they connected the combination of speech and arm-movement with the sphere of Mars. This planet is not so intimately connected with the earth as is the moon, nor is that which underlies the foundation of speech and arm-organization so intimately connected with earthly man as is that which underlies the abdominal and leg-organization. In a certain sense we can say that the activity corresponding to the lower limbs works very strongly upon our unconscious realm. What corresponds to the arms and hands, however, works very powerfully upon our semi-conscious realm. It is indeed a fact that no one with wholly unskilled hands, no one wholly unable to perform any dexterous movements with the fingers, can be a very subtle thinker. He would in a sense seek a coarse thought-mesh rather than fine links of thought. If he has coarse, clumsy hands, he is much more qualified for materialism than one whose hand movements are more adroit. This has nothing to do with having an abstract conception of the universe, but with the true inclination to a spiritual view of the universe, which always demands to be comprehended in finely meshed thoughts.

All these matters are taken fully into consideration in a pedagogy that encompasses the whole human being. You would probably be very pleased if you came to our Waldorf School and visited the classroom where, from ten o'clock, instruction is given in handicrafts. You would see the boys as well as the girls industriously absorbed in knitting or crochet. These things are the outcome of the whole spirit of the Waldorf School, for it is not a question of writing sundry abstract curricula, but of paying serious attention to the fact that what is taught should proceed from true knowledge of the human being; that as a teacher one should know the great difference it makes to the thinking whether I understand how to move my fingers nimbly, whether I am able in ordinary circumstances to cross the middle finger over the first, or not. The movements of our fingers are to a great extent the teachers of the elasticity of our thinking. These things must be followed with understanding and discernment. It is comparatively easy to acquire facility in crossing the middle finger over the first, making a serpent entwining the Mercury Staff, but it is not so easy to do the same with the second and third toes. In this we see what great distinctions there are in the whole organization of man. It is very important to bear this in mind, for the construction of the foot is intimately connected with our whole human *earthly* nature. The organization of our hands raises us above earthly nature. We raise ourselves to the *super-earthly*. Ancient wisdom had an intuitive sense of this, for it said that our lower realm belonged to the moon, but that the part of us which raised itself above earthly nature belonged to Mars. Primordial wisdom felt the organization in the whole universe in the same way as we sense the organization within ourselves. Materialism, however, has come to a point of ignorance about the human being. Again and again I must emphasize that the tragedy of materialism is that it turns its attention to matter, and all the time understands nothing at all of matter but simply loses connection with material existence. For this reason materialism can only cause social harm; for the socialistic materialists, the Marxists, are as regards reality just talkers. This they have learnt from the middle classes, which have indulged in materialistic chatter for centuries; but the latter have not applied it to social forms and structure, remaining satisfied with half-truths. A spiritual philosophy of life will once more reveal the nature of man, not in the abstract, but in specific soul-spiritual terms, which can have a real effect on all areas of our human existence.

One cannot advance in these things without constantly turning to the other side of life; for this development which our organization manifests is twofold, in so far as our upper realm is a metamorphosis of the lower realm in our last earth-life. There is a point of time between death and rebirth when a complete reversal takes place, when the inner is turned to the outer, when what is present as the connection between the organization of the liver and that of the spleen is changed in the whole structure of its forces into what becomes our hearing organization when we are reborn. The whole of our lower organization reappears transformed. In our lower realm we have a certain relationship between the spleen and the liver. They slide into one another as it were. What is now the spleen slips right through the liver, and comes out, in a certain respect, on the other side, appearing again in our hearing organization. It is similar with the other organs. People say that proof should be given of repeated earth-lives. Well, the methods by which such proofs can be found have first to be created. Anyone who is able to observe the human head in the right way, possessing a sense for such observation, comes to understand the transformation of our lower realm into the human head; but he cannot understand this without taking account of the intermediate stages—of our experiences between death and rebirth.

In this connection we can experience some very remarkable things. It may perhaps astonish some of you when I say that an artist who has become well acquainted with our outlook said: 'All that anthroposophy says is very beautiful, but there is no proof. De Rochas, for instance, has given proofs, for he has shown how in certain conditions of hypnosis, memories of former earth-lives may arise.' It seemed strange to me that an artist of all people should have said such a thing. I might have replied by saying that this was the same as telling him: 'My dear friend, your pictures tell me nothing; show me first the original of them, then I will believe that they are good,' or something of the kind. That of course, would be nonsense. As soon as he leaves his own field of expertise, he has no power to understand how, out of what he has before him, out of the true form of the human head, one can arrive at what is expressed in this human head. The picture must speak through itself, not through a mere likeness to the original. The human head speaks for itself. It corresponds to reality. It is our transformed lower realm and points us back to a previous earth-life. One must however first develop in oneself the capacity to understand reality aright.

The physical is thus seen to be a direct expression of the spiritual. It is possible to understand physical man as an expression of the spiritual which is experienced between death and rebirth. The physical world explains itself and brings the spiritual world into this explanation. But we must first know this, saying to ourselves: The phenomena of nature are only half the story, as long as we relate to them as mere sense-phenomena. We must first know this. Then we can find the bridge and understand the event that gave earth its true meaning—the event of Golgotha. Then we can understand how a purely spiritual event can at the same time enter right into physical life. If a person is not prepared to see the relation of the physical to the spiritual aright, he will never be able to grasp the fact that the event of Golgotha is both a spiritual event and one that occurred on the physical plane. When at the eighth General Ecumenical Council, in the year 869, the spirit was 'abolished', it became impossible to understand the event of Golgotha. The interesting point is that while Western Churches started from Christianity, they took great care that the essence of Christianity should *not* be understood. For the nature and essence of Christianity must be grasped through the *spirit*. The Western creeds set themselves against the spirit, and one of the principal reasons why anthroposophy is scorned by the Roman Catholic Church is that it relinquishes the erroneous claim that 'man consists of soul and body', and returns to the truth that 'man consists of body, soul *and spirit*'. The fact that the Roman Catholic Church regards anthroposophy as taboo indicates the interest it has in preventing man from coming to knowledge of the spirit, and so arriving at the true significance of the event of Golgotha. Thus the knowledge which, as we see, throws so much light on an understanding of man's true being, has been entirely lost.

How then can we develop an education suitable for the humanity of today, when vision of the true nature of man has been lost? To be an educationalist means to solve those sublime riddles which the child presents to us, as it gradually brings forth what has become part of it between death and re-birth. The creeds, however, reckon only with life after death—in order to humour human egotism; they have *not* reckoned that human life on earth should be regarded as a continuation of heavenly life. To require that we should prove ourselves worthy of what was asked of us before we entered earthly life through birth requires a certain selflessness of view, whereas until now the creeds have chiefly reckoned with egotism. Here, in anthroposophy, whatever is of the nature of creed or faith gains, as it were, a moral colouring. Here purely theoretical knowledge is made to flow into a higher ethical view of the world. Friends of anthroposophy should understand this. They should understand that, in a sense, a moral inclination to spirituality is the preliminary condition for a knowledge of spiritual beings. In our present difficult time, it is especially necessary that attention should be paid to this moral aspect of our world view. If we examine what is taking place in the outer world, we must say that materialism has given rise to empty talk, the sister of falsehood, even as far as man's ethical experience is concerned. This would become worse and worse if humanity were not helped by knowledge which leads to the spirit, and which must be united with a raising of our inner moral sense. We ought to acquire a realization of how a spiritual-scientific conception of the world relates to the tasks and the whole dignity of man, and we should take this sense as a starting point of our knowledge. This is only too necessary for mankind today, and one would like to find new phrases, new forms of expression in which to describe this aspect of the task of spiritual science!

Lecture 10

To understand the world without understanding man is impossible. That is the net result to be derived from our studies here. And for that very reason I wish today to contribute a little more to an understanding of man. Let us then start from the disparity between the organization of the head and that of the limb realm—a subject on which we have already frequently spoken here.

First of all I would remind you that the head-organization, as it appears in the life between birth and death, is the outcome of all those formative processes which have been at work from the previous death to the earthly embodiment of this present life. From this we must conclude that everything connected with the head-organization does not follow those laws and forces to which we are adapted as *earthly* beings. Through the bodily organization which we receive in this particular incarnation we are adapted to earth-life. We have spoken a little of how this manifests. We complete one cycle, of taking nourishment and digesting it, every 24 hours. Thus the cycle of nourishment and digestion is related to the movement of the earth in 24 hours. Something is accomplished in us that, as it were, resembles what the earth accomplishes within the universe. But our head is something whose organization we more or less bring with us at birth; therefore the head is primarily adjusted not to earthly relationships, but to such as are really from *beyond the earth*. The head is thus in a peculiar situation in relation to the rest of man. A comparison may serve to make clear the situation of man's head during the early epochs of his life on earth.

Suppose we were on board a ship. The ship makes various movements in different directions. If we have a compass, we see that the position of the magnetic needle does not follow the movement of the ship, but points always to the magnetic North Pole. It is independent of the movements of the ship. In fact the ship's movements can themselves be guided by the constant position of the magnetic needle. In a sense it is the same with the human head. Man does many things in the physical world with the rest of his organism; the head in a sense has no part in what he does in earthly life. Its inborn forces are always organized in accordance with the super-earthly. It is a very important fact that we have in the human head something organized in relation to what is super-earthly. Nevertheless there is always an interaction between the organization of the head and that of the rest of man. This interaction is only gradually brought to completion in the course of the time that passes between birth and death. The head, as we receive it from the super-earthly worlds at birth, is organized primarily for the life of ideation. It is in a sense so constructed that the life of ideas can use it as an instrument. If it were to develop only on the basis of the forces which it receives on leaving the super-earthly worlds, it would develop solely as an organ of ideation or thought; our connection with the world through the head-organization would in course of time be entirely lost. We should, as it were, so pass through earthly life with our consciousness as to develop ideas alone by means of the head—that is, no more than pictures of earthly life. We should become more and more conscious of extending beyond our earth-related organization, of extending beyond it with our head; as though through our head we were beings who were strange to the earth and developed only pictures of all that is connected with earthly life.

This is not so, and precisely for the reason that the rest of the organism sends its forces into the head. If we enquire into the quality of these forces, which from childhood onwards are more and more directed from the rest of the organism into the head, if we wish to describe them, we must look for them particularly in the forces of will. The rest of the organism is continually impregnating the thought-nature of the head with will-forces. Thus we can say, in effect, speaking diagrammatically, that we acquire the head as the bearer of ideas, as the result of the foregoing incarnation; while the will-forces are sent into it from the rest of the organism. What has just been said takes place not only in the life of soul, but shows its effects in physical terms too.

Inasmuch as we bring head forces with us we are born in this earthly world as beings of thought and ideation, and the forces of ideation are at first very powerful. They ray out from the head into the rest of the organism, and it is they which during the first seven years of life enable the forces which manifest in the second dentition to work out of the rest of our organism. These same forces consolidate in us also the life of thought, which is not consolidated until we acquire the second teeth. They are the actual forces which produce the teeth; so that when we have the teeth, these forces are set free, and can assert themselves in the life of ideas. They can then form clearly defined concepts, and build the power of memory. Clearly outlined ideas can begin to find a place in our thought. As long however as we are employing these forces in the formation of the teeth, they cannot show themselves as true consolidating forces in the life of ideas.

As we grow beyond the seventh or eighth year, the will, which is essentially bound up with our lower realm and not with the head, begins to manifest; and now comes the time when it would, as it were, shoot its forces up into the head. This cannot however come about so easily; for our head, which is organized in relation to what is super-earthly, would not be able directly to receive these strong forces which try to ascend from the metabolic system, as vehicle of the will. These forces must first be stemmed; they must make a halt until sufficiently filtered, toned down, given more of a 'soul' character, to make their influence felt in the head. This halt is made at the end of the second seven-year period, when the will-forces are arrested in the organization of the *larynx*—for that is the way they manifest. In the male organization they suddenly break forth in the change of voice. In the female organization they manifest differently. These are the will forces coming to a standstill, as it were, before they reach the head. Thus we may say that at the end of our second seven-year period, the will forces are arrested in the speech organization. At that time they are sufficiently filtered and 'souled' to make their influence felt in the head-organization. Having reached the age of puberty, and the change of voice which runs parallel with it, we have reached the point when through the head the faculty of thought and ideation can work together with the will.

Here we have an example of how our spiritual science can give real insight into actual phenomena. The abstract philosophies which make their influence felt in modern times— Schopenhauer's *The World as Will and Idea* for instance—all remain abstract. Schopenhauer took pains to describe the world in its ideal character on the one hand, and its will character on the other; but he remains merely abstract. So also does Eduard von Hartmann. They all remain abstract. To be concrete is to observe how, through these two stages— at the first and second seven-year periods—idea and will meet in quite definite and distinct ways in the cosmic system of the human head. The essential thing is that we can point to the way soul and spirit manifest; and at the same time how in the outer physical world the forces of the head sent forth to the body manifest in the forming of the teeth. These work together with the forces of the body ascending into the head, which prepare themselves, through first arresting themselves in speech and only then shooting into the head, to become true soul-will.

Thus we must understand human development, and look at what actually goes on in man. I have said that the human head is no more adjusted to our earthly circumstances than is the magnetic needle to the movements of the ship. The needle is independent of them, and the human head is in the same way independent of earthly circumstances.

Here we have something which gradually leads to the *physiological concept of freedom.* Here we have the physiology of what I have set forth in my *Philosophy of Spiritual Activity,* namely, that one can only understand freedom by grasping it in sense-free thinking—that is to say, in the processes taking place in us when we direct pure thinking through our will and orientate it according to certain defined directions.

So you see how one can gradually come to a real investigation of the mutual relationship between soul-spiritual and physical nature, and how the process of speech development can be really understood by conceiving of it as a product of two sources supplying the human being, those in our head-realm on the one hand, and in the limb realm on the other.

We can now experience more fully how impossible it is to say that some kind of communication of the will is carried from the brain through the motor nerves. The brain only derives its full power of volition from the rest of the organism. Of course you are not to imagine this as if you could draw it in a diagram, for the process that in a certain sense arrests itself in speech development is something arising earlier, which goes through the whole of life, and whose most characteristic features only appear at special times of transition. Thus we must understand clearly how man is adapted to both an *earthly* and a *super-earthly* life.

He is adapted to earthly life in such a way that he does not bring to conclusion in his purely natural organization certain forces which the animal does bring to their conclusion. The animal is, as it were, born ready-equipped for all its functions. Man has to be taught to acquire these functions for himself.

What thus takes place in man is really only an outer expression of something that takes place in him organically. If we study the metabolism of the animal correctly, we find that it goes further than that of man. The metabolism of man must be held back at an earlier stage. What in the animal is carried to a certain stage must in man be arrested at an earlier stage. Superficially expressed, man does not carry digestion so far as the animal; the digestive process ceases earlier. He retains, through this arrested digestion, forces which become the vehicle for what he sends to the head through the will.

As you see, human nature is complicated; and if one does not wish to take the trouble really to study its complexity— why then, one arrives at a science such as we have in the external science of today! One does not arrive at the real nature of man. The essential nature of man will only be revealed when spiritual science is allowed to illuminate natural science. If, however, man is organized in the way I have described, and the connection between man and the extra-human world outside him is as we have described it in these studies, then you will see that the extra-human world can only exist for man if it has a certain resemblance to him, to his organization. We have seen that our limb realm adapts us to earthly relationships, but that through the head-organization we remove ourselves as it were from earthly relations, like the ship's compass on the ship. Now something of this kind must take place also in the extra-human world. There must, for instance, be something in the planetary movements that corresponds to the adaptation of our human limb-nature. Something must therefore lift itself out beyond earthly conditions, there must be something that does not belong.

How does modern natural science study man? It studies him as though he had no head. Of course it studies the head too, but how? As a kind of appendage to the rest of his organism. What natural science produces for the comprehension of human nature is only suited for explaining the part outside the head, not the human head itself; that can be understood only in terms of the spiritual world.

I might have used the following comparison. I might have said—I have already spoken of it recently—that the human head sits upon the rest of the human organism as people sit in a railway carriage. They take no personal part in the movement. They sit still and allow the carriage to move. In the same way, the human head sits at ease. It regards the rest of the organism, which is adapted to the outer world, as its coach, and allows itself to be carried. It is itself organized for a very different world. And this must correspond to something in the outer world also. A natural history of man, such as we have today, really speaks of a headless man, it does not understand his true nature at all. And an astronomy constructed on the same principles would not correspond to the whole super-earthly world, but only to a certain part of it; the other part not included under this aspect, is not considered at all. As a matter of fact the trend of natural science for the last three or four centuries has been such that it deduced the movements of the universe, without taking a certain content of this universe into account, just as the rest of natural science disregards the human head. Therefore astronomy has derived forms of movements such as 'The earth revolves in an elliptical path round the sun', which are as little correct for the universe as the natural science of today is for man's whole being. They do not correspond to the actual facts. Hence we must so often point out that the Copernican view must be made fruitful through spiritual science. Many mystics, and theosophists too, are fond of preaching that the world of senses around us is 'maya'. But they do not draw the ultimate logical conclusion, otherwise they would have to say: 'Even the world of the Copernican system, this movement of the earth around the sun is maya, is an illusion, and must be revised.' For we must realize that it contains something which can no more be recognized in terms of the hypothesis employed by Copernicus, Galileo—or even Kepler—than the whole nature of man can be understood through modern scientific principles.

Now when we come to discuss a subject like this, we must at the same time point to something which has already taken place in human evolution. If we call to mind what we have often said—that in olden times there was a kind of primeval wisdom of which man had but a dreamy atavistic conscious-ness, but which in its content far surpassed what we have since acquired—if we remember all this, we shall not find it difficult to bear in mind also that the world view which was held in olden times was quite different from any cosmology possible today. For what was the cosmology of our forefathers—that is, of ourselves in our former earth-lives? What was it?

The cosmology that man had in those times consisted far more than it does now in what he brought into the world at physical birth. We may still find in children, if we understand how to observe them aright, something like a picture of the world in which man lived before descending to physical life. In later life however, and indeed from quite an early stage, this picture vanishes. In olden times this picture endured. What existed in earlier epochs of spiritual evolution as an astro-nomical description of the solar or planetary system and its relation to man was something man felt within him, although he experienced it in a dream-like state. Today we look back upon those times of our ancestors with a certain arrogance, yet they were times when we really knew there was something within ourselves that had a connection with Mars, Mercury, and so on. That was part of the inner consciousness of the human being. It disappeared however as man evolved further. In primeval times he not only saw the outer constellation, but felt within himself an inner constellation, an *inner cosmic sys-tem*. Not only did he perceive a cosmic system outside him; but in his own head, which today is merely the vehicle of the— shall I say—indefinite life of ideas, there within shone the sun, with the planets circling round. In his head man carried this cosmic picture, and it had an inner force which worked upon the rest of the organism and influenced what he received at birth, or rather at conception, from earthly forces; the rest of man's organism was influenced, and drawn into this adaptation to the planetary forces.

And now we can carry the thought a little further. Man is born into this world, and as a heritage he receives—let us say—in the first place, the power to acquire his teeth, the milk-teeth. These develop roughly within the first year. The second teeth need seven times as long; they are brought forth by the human organism itself. This points in the deepest sense to the fact that a certain rhythm which we bring with us at birth and which relates to the yearly revolution is slowed down by seven times in our earthly life. By seven times is the yearly revolution slowed down, and this is expressed in the fact that man has introduced into his division of time the relation of one to seven—day and week. The week is seven times as long as the day. This is an expression of how something takes its course in man which goes seven times slower than what he brings into physical existence at birth. Man will not understand the actual processes in the human being until he is able to see quite clearly and exactly how something within him which, as it were, is brought with him from conditions outside the earth, has to be slowed down by seven times during the earthly period.

Ancient Mystery teaching spoke much of these facts. If I were to express in our language what the old Hebrew Mystery teachings, for example, said from their atavistic knowledge of these matters, I should have to put it in this way: Jehovah, who is the true earth god, who added the earth-organization to that of Saturn, Sun and Moon, has the tendency to slow down seven times what comes from the moon-organization. In relation to the course of the earth something in the human being wants to go at accelerated speed. I might even say that the old Hebrew Mystery teacher said to his pupils: 'Lucifer runs seven times as fast as Jehovah.' This points to two movements, two currents in human nature. These two currents also exist in super-earthly nature—only there they are present in a somewhat different form. The thought however, which we here approach, is one not very easy to understand. We can perhaps gain insight into it by starting from social relationships, and then subsequently returning to cosmic-tellurian relationships.

I have often spoken in public lectures of something I should like to express here. When we contemplate the misery of the present time, we find the peculiar fact that the whole intelligence of modern humanity has developed in a way that is quite estranged from reality. It is a peculiar fact that, in practical life, we find more inefficient people than efficient. There is a good example of this in the fact that in the nineteenth century there was much discussion concerning the effect of the Gold Standard upon international economic relations. You can go through the parliamentary reports of that century, and try to form an idea from them of what people then thought would be the result of monometalism, the Gold Standard. They regarded it as something which would make free trade possible unhindered by imposition of duty. Throughout the united economic domains of the world this was predicted wherever the Gold Standard was extolled. What has actually come about? The imposition of duty. Little by little the actual relations have developed in such a way that everywhere duties have been imposed. That is the actual outcome.

Judging superficially one might say: Well, those people must have been very stupid! But they were not at all stupid; among those who had pledged themselves to the promotion of free trade by the Gold Standard were very able and clever persons, but they had no sense of reality, they reckoned only according to logic. They could not enter into the true circumstances and relationships, any more than can our modern scientists comprehend the organization of the heart, liver, spleen and so on. They make abstract theories and hold on to them; although they are materialists they remain rooted in the abstract. That is why such an occurrence is possible as that related in the following anecdote, which is founded on fact and is really very illuminating.

In a certain scientific academy there was a physiologist, a learned man, who developed a theory about the varying length of time particular birds can fast. He drew up a beautiful schedule. He had large cages of birds placed in his corridor and he starved those birds to ascertain how long they could live without food. He registered the times and obtained some lovely big numbers as a result. He elaborated these in a paper which he read at a meeting of the academy. Now in the same house there lived, on the floor above, another physiologist who did not apply the same methods. After the learned treatise had been read, he rose and said: 'I must unfortunately object that these figures are not correct, for I had such pity on the poor birds that I fed them in passing.' Now things do not always have to happen just like this! This is an anecdote. But it is founded on fact; and really much of the material underlying our exact science has been obtained in a similar way. Someone in the background has 'fed the birds' instead of their having starved as long as the schedule showed. If one has a sense for reality, one cannot very well work with statistical methods of that kind; they do not hold out much promise. But this sense for reality is wholly lacking in modern humanity. Why is this so? It is due to a certain necessity of the evolution of humanity; and we can understand the matter as follows.

Picture it to yourselves in this way. The man of ancient times looked into this outer world. By means of all that he bore within him, he viewed the relationships and connections of the world outside. He also formed his theory of the stars out of his own inner stellar system. He had 'a sense for reality' and he carried it in his senses. This sense for reality has disappeared in the course of man's evolution. It will have to be developed again, it will have to be developed to the same degree inwardly as it formerly was outwardly. We must really cultivate this sense for reality in our inner being by the training we receive in spiritual science; only then shall we be able to develop it in the world outside. If man were to keep straight on evolving in the modern intellectual way, he would at length be quite unable to perceive what is going on around him, and then it could easily happen that while the cry 'Free Trade is coming!' goes up, in reality customs restrictions will be established. Something similar is continually happening in the various domains of so-called practical life. What happened then on a large scale happens today in small things everywhere. The 'practical' person predicts one thing, the opposite happens. It would be interesting to keep an acount of what 'practical' people predicted as 'certain to happen' during the last years of the war. Always the opposite came about, especially in the later years, precisely because people no longer had any sense for reality. This sense, however, can arise in no other way than by developing it within us first. In future times no one will be considered a practical man, or a thinker attuned to reality, who disdains to educate his inner being through spiritual science, in a manner in which the outer world cannot educate us today. We must carry into the world outside what we develop within. Hence the need for spiritual science; for people cannot determine the relation of the heart to the liver if they do not first acquire the method to do so by means of a training in spiritual science. In former times people could say: The heart is related to the liver somewhat as the sun to Mercury in the outer world; and man knew something of how this relationship of the sun to Mercury was drawn from the super-sensible world into the sense world. This is now no longer understood, nor can it ever be thoroughly understood if the foundation, the basic impulse for this comprehension, be not acquired from within. It is not through clairvoyance alone that man can make it his own. By clairvoyance the facts of spiritual science are investigated; but man acquires this sense when he enters with his whole thought and feeling into what has already been discovered by clairvoyant methods, and regulates his life accordingly. That is the essential point. What is of importance is *to study the conclusions of spiritual science*, not to satisfy a curiosity for clairvoyance. That must be emphasized again and again. For in the whole development of human culture, this application of the methods of spiritual science to outer life and to the knowledge of the wider world, the world outside us, is of quite special importance.

When we consider what we thus have to regard as our original head-organization, when we consider it in the course of our life, we see how it gradually becomes permeated with everything in our organization that is adapted to the outside world. Thus we must learn to understand the world outside man through man's own organism, through our human limb-organization; and there only such things as I have already hinted at can help us. I have shown the contrast that exists between our waking and sleeping conditions. These are contrasting conditions, and when one condition passes over into the other, that is to say, when we wake up and when we go to sleep, then we pass through a kind of zero-point of our existence, a sort of needle's eye. The moment of awaking and the moment of falling asleep must have something to do with one another.

This indicates that if we try to turn man's daily cycle into a geometrical figure, we can employ neither a circle nor an ellipse; for if we were to ascribe to the sleep condition one part of the ellipse, the conditions of awaking and falling asleep would be sundered; and this they cannot be. We shall see how even in outer appearance they present a similarity and cannot be sundered. Thus we cannot draw the geometrical figure which is to correspond with man's daily round in a circular form nor in an elliptic form. We can only draw it as a looped line, a lemniscate. When we say that man falls asleep passing from the waking condition into the sleep condition, then with the lemniscate it is possible to show him coming out of sleep again, passing through the same point; and then we have a curving line, which truly corresponds to the daily course of human life. There is no other line for the daily course of life than the lemniscate, for no other line would lead our awakening through the same point as our falling asleep.

There is more than this. If we give attention to human development, in childhood especially, we have to say: we wake up virtually the same as we went to sleep. But if we rightly observe life, we cannot exclude the sleeping condition from human life as a whole. We instruct our children during the day. Out of all we bring to the child, much of it is not his at once, but becomes so only the next day, after the ego and astral body have passed through the night-condition; only then does the child duly receive what we have given him by day. We must always have this in mind and regulate our teaching and education accordingly. Thus in regard to the alternating condition of day and night, we can say: we sleep, and on awaking return to the same place where we fell asleep; but in regard to human development, we shall have to say: we advance a little each time. In a different sense we progress.

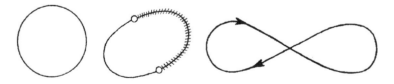

Hence we may not draw the line quite as a lemniscate; but in such a way that we return to waking life a little further on, and so attain a *progressive* lemniscate (A). Thus when we observe the alternating conditions of waking and sleeping,

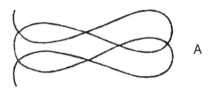

A

and continue the development, we obtain a spiral. This spiral is ultimately connected with our evolution, and our evolution again is connected with the whole cosmic system. Therefore we must seek this same line as the basis of the movements of the universe. If, instead of abstract geometry, man had applied concrete geometry to celestial space, the concrete geometry that proceeds from a study of the whole human being, he would have arrived at something different. For in ancient wisdom one had this line (B). And one did not speak of Mars as moving along any other kind of line than this one. Gradually it was all forgotten. Man began to *calculate* instead of knowing. What was the result? People could no longer continue along this kind of line.

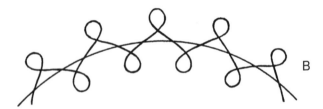

B

Instead they took this line and set circles upon it (C) and acquired the epicycloid theory. The Ptolemaic theory is the last remnant of ancient primeval wisdom. Copernicus further simplified it, and modern astronomy still bases its specu-

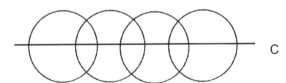

C

lations on that today—but in such a way that it much prefers to consider ellipses and circles than that inwardly alive line which presents an advancing spiral. Then people wonder that their observations do not agree with their calculations, and that fresh corrections continually have to be made.

Reflect how the whole theory of relativity has been constructed on an error in Mercury's period of orbit. But people attempt to correct this in a different way than would have been the case if one had gone back to man's relation to the whole cosmos. Of this more in the next lecture.

Lecture 11

I drew attention yesterday to the fact that what is present in man points to something correspondingly present in the cosmos outside him. And now I would like to give special attention to the relation of our head to a world beyond the earth—a world that lies beyond the world upon which the rest of the human organism is dependent. The head points clearly to the world through which we passed between death and rebirth, its whole organization being so modelled that it forms a distinct echo of our sojourn in the spiritual world. Now let us look for the corresponding phenomenon in the cosmos.

We need only compare the behaviour of Saturn, which stands far out in the universe, with that of the earth to notice a certain difference. Astronomy recognizes this difference by saying that Saturn goes round the sun in 30 years, while the earth goes round it in one year. We will not stop now to discuss whether these claims are correct or whether they are one-sided. We will only point to the fact that the observation gained by following Saturn in cosmic space and comparing the rapidity of its progress with that of the earth brings us to the conclusion that, in the astronomical system of Copernicus and Kepler, Saturn needs 30 years and the earth only one year to go round the sun. To Jupiter we assign a revolution lasting 12 years. Much shorter is that of Mars. And when we come to the other planets, Venus and Mercury, we find that they have even shorter periods of orbit than the earth. All these conclusions are obviously well thought out, worked out on the basis of observations made in one way or another.

I have pointed out that we only gain a clear insight into

these things by comparing what takes place in the far distances of cosmic space with what goes on within the boundary of our skin, in our own organism. Reflect for a moment and you will find that what is called the period of the earth's revolution round the sun corresponds to something in yourself. In the foregoing lecture we showed that in order to represent the daily course of our lives we have to use a certain curving line that turns back upon itself. In a similar way must the curved line corresponding to the yearly motion of the earth be imagined, irrespective of whether we think that the movement of the earth is at the same time a movement round the sun or not; for what have we here? Let us think. We have our own daily cycle of life, which we will consider now, not in its correspondence to the cosmos, but as it presents itself in us, so that we can also include those whose sleeping and waking do not correspond with the alternation of day and night— idlers as well as all those who live irregular lives! Let us consider this daily round of man on the basis already established, that is to say, representing it in thought as a line in which the points of sleeping and waking are superimposed, as I have pointed out. There are many reasons, but one will suffice to show that we are bound to superimpose the point of waking over that of falling asleep. Consider the remarkable fact that when we look back over our life, it appears to us as an unbroken stream. We do not feel compelled to regard life in such a way as to say: Today I have lived and have been conscious of my environment from the moment of waking; before that all was darkness; before that again, my falling asleep of yesterday was preceded by living, waking experience, back to the moment of waking; but then darkness again. You do not picture the stream of memory like this, you picture it so that the moment of awaking and the moment of falling asleep really unite in your conscious recollection. That is a plain fact. This fact can be expressed in that the curve representing our daily cycle comes out as a spiral, with the point of awaking always crossing the point of falling asleep. If the curve were an ellipse or a circle, then awaking and falling asleep would have to be separate, they could not possibly be superimposed. In this way alone therefore can we picture our daily cycle.

Now let us try to see exactly what this means for us. Your waking time runs from your awaking to your falling asleep. During that time you are a physical human being, and you are moreover a *complete* human being, possessing physical body, etheric body, astral body and ego. Now consider your condition from falling asleep until awaking. Then you have only physical body and etheric body. As physical human being you are not a human being as such; you have only physical body and etheric body. Strictly speaking, such a thing should not be. Your physical body and etheric body become really an untruth, for a being so composed should be a plant. It is the remainder of the whole human being, left behind when the ego and astral body have departed; and only by virtue of the fact that these will return before the physical and etheric bodies can actually reach the plant stage—it is only because of this that you do not die every night.

Now let us examine what is left lying on the bed. What happens to it? It suddenly becomes plant-like. Its life is comparable to what takes place on earth from the moment when plants sprout in spring until the autumn, when they die down. This plant-nature springs up and puts forth leaf in man, so to say, from falling asleep to awaking. He is then like the earth in summer; and when the ego and astral body return and man awakes, he becomes like the earth in winter. So that we may say that the time between awaking and falling asleep is our winter, and that between falling asleep and awaking is our summer. For the year of the cosmos—in so far as the earth is part of it—corresponds with man's day. The earth wakes in winter and sleeps in summer. The summer is the earth's sleeping time, the winter its waking time. Outer perception obviously gives a false analogy, presenting summer as the

earth's waking time and winter as its time of sleeping. The
reverse is the case, for during sleep we resemble blossoming,
sprouting plant-life, like the earth in summer. When our ego
and astral body re-enter our physical and etheric bodies, it is
as though the summer sun withdrew from the plant-laden
earth and the winter sun began to work. Thus the whole year
is at different times represented in any one part of the earth's
surface. The case of the earth is different from that of an
individual human being, but only apparently so. In whichever
part of the earth we may dwell, a year's course corresponds to
the daily course of an individual human being. The course of a
year in the cosmos corresponds to a person's day.

Thus we have the direct fact that when we look up to the
cosmos we have to say: A year—that is for the cosmos sleeping
and waking; and if our earth is the head of the cosmos, it
expresses the waking of the cosmos in winter, and its sleeping
in summer. If we now consider the cosmos, which as we see
manifests waking and sleeping—for the plant-covering of the
earth is an outcome of cosmic working—we shall find that we
have to think of it as a great organism. We must think of what
takes place in its constituent parts as organically integrated
into the whole cosmos, just as what takes place in one of our
own organs is integrated into our organism. And here we
come to the significance of what astronomy expresses as the
difference between the shorter periods of Venus' and Mercury's revolutions in comparison with the longer periods of
Mars, Jupiter and Saturn. When we consider the so-called
outer planets, Saturn, Jupiter and Mars, then Sun, Mercury,
Venus and Earth, we find this apparently long period of
revolution in the case of the outer planets stretching beyond a
year, thus beyond mere waking time. Let us consider Saturn
with its 30-year orbit of the sun. How can we express these
apparent 30 years in the language of the cosmos, whose year is
its daily cycle? If a year is the daily cycle of the cosmos, then
the apparent period of Saturn's revolution is approximately

30 days, a cosmic month, a cosmic four weeks. Thus we may say that if we regard Saturn as the outermost planet (the other two, Uranus and Neptune, regarded today as of equal significance with Saturn, are really additions from without), then we must say that Saturn bounds our cosmos; and, in its apparent slowness, in its limping behind the earth, we behold the four-weekly, or monthly, cycle of the cosmos compared to the life it displays in the course of our year, which for the cosmos is like a falling asleep and awaking.

From this it may be seen that Saturn, if its apparent path is regarded as the outermost limit of our planetary system, is inwardly related to the latter in a different way from, let us say, Mercury; Mercury, needing less than 100 days for its apparent revolution, moves quickly, is inwardly active, has a certain celerity, whereas Saturn moves slowly.

To what exactly does this correspond? In the movement of Saturn you have something comparatively slow, in that of Mercury something that is very much quicker, an inner activity of the cosmic organism, something that stirs the cosmos inwardly. It is as if you had, let us say, a kind of living, mucilaginous organism, itself revolving, but having also within it an organ which is revolving more quickly. Mercury separates itself from the movement of the whole by its quicker revolution. It is, as it were, an enclosed member; so too is the movement of Venus. Here we have something analogous to the relation of our head to the rest of our organism. The head separates itself off from the movements of the rest of the organism. Venus and Mercury emancipate themselves from the movement set by Saturn. They go their own way; they vibrate within the whole system. What does this signify? They have something extra as compared with the whole system; their more rapid movement shows this. What corresponds in our head to this extra aspect? Our head has something extra, namely, its orientation to the supersensible world; but our head is at rest in our organism, just as we are at rest in a coach or a railway carriage, while it is moving. Venus and Mercury act differently; they do the exact opposite as regards their emancipation. Whereas our head is quiescent, as we are when we sit still in a railway carriage, Venus and Mercury emancipate themselves from the whole planetary system in the opposite way. It is as though we, sitting in the railway carriage, were impelled by something to move all the time much faster than the train itself. This is due to the fact that Venus and Mercury, with their much quicker apparent movement, are related not to space alone, but to that to which our head is also related; only these relations take opposite courses—our head being brought to rest, Venus and Mercury on the other hand becoming more active. They are the two planets through which our planetary system has a relation to the supersensible world. They incorporate our planetary system into the cosmos in a different way than do Jupiter and Saturn. Our planetary system is spiritualized through Venus and Mercury, more intimately adapted to the spiritual powers than happens through Jupiter and Saturn.

Things that are real often appear quite differently when studied according to true reality instead of according to generally received opinion. Just as, when we judge externally, we call winter the sleeping time of the earth, and summer its waking time, whereas the reverse is true. In the same way, judging externally, Saturn and Jupiter might be regarded as more spiritual than Venus and Mercury. This is not the case; for Venus and Mercury stand in more intimate relation to something underlying the whole cosmos than do Jupiter and Saturn. Thus we may say that in Venus and Mercury we have something which places us outwardly, as a member of the planetary system, in relation to a supersensible world. Here, while we live on earth, we are brought into connection with a supersensible world through Venus and Mercury. We might say: When we are incorporated by birth into the physical world, we are carried into it by Saturn and Jupiter; while we live from birth to death, Venus and Mercury work within us and prepare us to carry our supersensible part back again through death into the supersensible world. In fact, Mercury and Venus have just as much share in our immortality *after* death as Jupiter and Saturn have in our life *before* death. It is really so, we have to see something in the cosmos which corresponds to the relation between the comparatively more spiritual organization of the head and the rest of the human organization.

Now let us suppose that Saturn also pursues its movement in a similar curve (lemniscate)—only, of course, its path is different through cosmic space, having a movement 30 times less rapid than the earth; if we picture these two curves, we must realize that each planetary body which follows such a path (lemniscate) is obviously moved in this path by forces, but each one by forces of a different kind. Then we come to an idea which is extremely important and which, if taken rightly, will probably at once strike you as true. If it does not, it is only because, under the influence of the materialism of the last centuries, people are not accustomed to connect such things with the facts of the universe.

To the modern materialistic view of the cosmos, Saturn is observed merely as a body moving about in cosmic space; and the same with the other planets. This is not the case; for if we take Saturn, the outermost planet of our universe, we must represent it as the *leader* of our planetary system in cosmic space. Saturn directs our system in space, embodying that

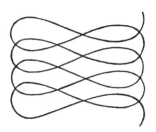

outermost force which draws us round in the lemniscate in cosmic space. Saturn is simultaneously both the driver and the horse, the force at the outermost periphery of our solar system. If Saturn worked alone, we should continually move solely in a lemniscate. But there are other forces in our planetary system which show a more intimate mediation with the spiritual world—the forces that we find in Mercury and Venus. Through these forces our path is continually raised. Thus, when we look upon the path from above, we have the lemniscate, but when we look at it sideways, we obtain lines which are continually rising upwards; there is a progression. This progression corresponds in man to the fact that, during sleep, what we have taken into us, though it may not pass over at once into consciousness, is worked upon and deepened; during sleep we work upon it. It is principally during sleep that we work on what we have absorbed through our life and education. During sleep Mercury and Venus communicate that to us. They are our most important night-planets, as Jupiter and Saturn are our most important day-planets. Hence ancient, instinctive atavistic wisdom was right in connecting Jupiter and Saturn with the formation of the human head, Mercury and Venus with the formation of the human trunk, with the rest of the organism. These things arose from an intimate knowledge of the connection between man and the universe.

Now I will ask you carefully to consider the following. It is first of all necessary to gain inner understanding of the earth's movement. We must recognize the influence upon it of Venus and Mercury forces, which bear the lemniscate further, so that it progresses, and its axis itself becomes a lemniscate. Thus for the earth we have an extremely complicated movement. And now I come to what I wish to point out. Suppose we have to draw this movement. Astronomy tries to do so. Astronomy wants to have a planetary system; it wants to draw the solar system and explain it by calculation. Planets such as Venus and Mercury, however, have relation to the extra-spatial, the supersensible, the spiritual, to that which does not originally belong in space, but has, as it were, come into it. Thus if you have the paths of Saturn, Jupiter, Mars, and in the same space also draw in the paths of Mercury and Venus, you will get at most a projection of the Mercury or of the Venus orbit, but in no sense the orbits themselves. If we employ three-dimensional space to sketch in the orbits of Jupiter, Saturn and Mars, we come at most to a boundary, where we get something like a path of the sun. But if we wish to draw the others, we can no longer do so in three-dimensional space, we can only obtain shadow-pictures of these other movements in it; we cannot draw the path of Venus and that of Saturn in the same three-dimensional space. From this we see that all delineations of the solar system where the same kind of space is used for Saturn as for Venus are only approximate, they do not suffice for a solar system. Such drawings are as little possible as it would be to explain the whole being of man according to purely natural forces only. This shows why no depiction of the solar system is adequate. A non-astronomer such as Johannes Schlaf was easily able to prove to quite well-established astronomers the impossibility of their solar system by very simple facts, pointing out that if the sun and the earth are so related that the latter revolves round the former, the sun-spots could not show themselves as they do, the earth being at various times in different positions relative to the sun, now behind it, now in front, now coming round again. That, however, is not the case at all. No drawing of our solar system that is inscribed into *one* space of the ordinary three dimensions will be right. We must understand this. Just as to understand man as a whole we must pass from physical to supersensible forces; so in the same way, to understand the solar-system, we must pass from three dimensions into other dimensions. That is to say, we cannot describe the ordinary solar system in terms of three-dimensional space alone.

Planetary 'globes' and so forth we have to look at as follows. If here we have Saturn on the globe and there Mercury, then it is not the true Mercury but its shadow only, its projection.

These are things that spiritual science must bring to light. They have quite faded from people's knowledge. About six or seven centuries before the Christian era, ancient primordial wisdom began gradually to disappear, until replaced by philosophy from the middle of the fifteenth century. But people such as Pythagoras, for instance, still knew so much of the ancient wisdom that they could say: We dwell on the earth, we belong through the earth to a cosmic system, to which Jupiter and Saturn also belong; but if we remain in these three dimensions, then we shall not belong in the same way to Venus and Mercury. We cannot belong to the two latter directly, as we do to Saturn and Jupiter; but if our earth is in one kind of space with Saturn and Jupiter, there must be a *'counter-earth'* which is in another space, with Venus and Mercury. Hence ancient astronomers spoke of the earth and the counter-earth. Of course the modern materialist would say: 'Counter-earth? I see nothing of that!' He is like a person who weighs another person, having first charged the other to think about nothing; and weighs him again when he has charged him to think a specially clever thought, and then says: I have weighed him, but I have not found the weight of his thought. Materialism rejects what has no weight or cannot be seen. Remarkable things however shine out of atavistic, primeval wisdom to which we can return through the inner vision of spiritual science. It is of urgent necessity that we should work our way through now to what is entirely new— which, however, was once known of long ago—for in our time it needs to be acquired in full consciousness. Unless we do this we shall lose the very possibility of thinking.

I called attention yesterday to the fact that a certain kind of thinking about social issues leads people to strive for 'monometallism', for the sake of free trade—and yet a protective tariff comes! No true social order will arise out of what is being striven for on the foundation of thinking people possess today; a true social order can only come about through thinking trained in a science which does not draw a planisphere showing Saturn and Venus in the same space. For the view of the universe which we are giving here does not merely mean that we hold something up before us, but also that, in a sense, we *learn to think*. What exactly does this mean?

Remember what I have said: when our bodily organization is remodelled in the next incarnation, it not only goes through a change, but is turned inside out. As a glove is turned from a left-hand to a right-hand glove by turning it inside out, so too what is now inside—liver, heart, kidneys—becomes the outer sense-organs: eye, ear and so on. It is all turned inside out. This corresponds to another turning inside out: Saturn on the one hand; and wholly outside its space, Venus and Mercury. A reversal within itself. If we do not observe this, what happens? It is the same as failing to observe the turning inside out in the case of the human head. When we do not observe the universe according to this law of reversal we do something very peculiar; we do not think with our head at all! And this is something to which the fifth post-Atlantean epoch is tending, in so far as it is descending and not seeking to ascend again by means of spiritual science. Man would like to wrest his head free and think only with the rest of the organism; that mode of thought is abstract. He wants to set the head free. He has no desire to lay claim to what has resulted from foregoing incarnations. He wants to reckon only with the present one. People do not only wish to deny successive earth-lives in theory. They carry their head, as it were, with outer dignity, because it sits like a lord over the rest of the organism, like a man riding in a carriage. But they do not take that rider in the carriage seriously; they carry him about with them, but make no claim upon his innate capacities. They make no practical use of their repeated earth-lives.

This tendency has been developing more or less since the beginning of the fifth post-Atlantean epoch, and we can only oppose it by taking up spiritual science. One might even define spiritual science as something that induces us to take our head seriously once more! From one point of view the essential aspect of spiritual science is really that it takes the human head seriously, not merely regarding it as an additional appendage to the rest of the organism. Europe especially, as it so rapidly approaches barbarism, would like to get rid of the head. Spiritual science must disturb this sleep. It must urge human beings to use their heads! This can only be done by taking the belief in repeated earth-lives seriously.

One cannot talk of spiritual science in the way that is usually done, if one takes it seriously. One must say what *is*; and to what is belongs something which appears as sheer madness, the fact that people disown their heads. They would rather not believe this, they prefer to regard truth as madness. This has always been so. Things in human evolution come about in such a way that people are taken unawares by the new. And so they must of course be shocked and astonished by this emphasis on the necessity for using the head. Lenin and Trotsky's message amounts to saying: 'Do not use your head, just use the rest of your organism.' The rest of the organism is a vehicle of the instincts. People are to be led by instincts alone. And they do this too, they carry it into their practice. It is their practice that nothing that arises from the human head should enter modern Marxist theories. These things are very serious—*how* serious they are has to be emphasized again and again.

Lecture 12

You will remember that I have discussed in detail how much criticism has come from many sides of the idea of a connection between the Christ event—the appearance of Christ on earth—and cosmic events such as the course of the sun, or the relation of the sun to the earth. The connection can only be understood when one studies more deeply all that we have hitherto said about the movements of the stellar system. Let us make a beginning in this direction today, for you will see that ultimately astronomy cannot really be studied at all without entering into a study of the whole being of man. I have already mentioned this, but we shall see how deeply grounded is the statement in the whole being of the world, for we can only understand something of the nature of the world or of the nature of man when we consider the two together, not separately, as is done at present. You will observe a curious fact in relation to this very matter, namely, that materialism, if only it is not directly acknowledged to be such, is preferred by the religious denominations to spiritual science. That is, both Protestants and Roman Catholics prefer to consider the outer world in its various realms in a materialistic sense, rather than to enquire how the spiritual works in the world and embodies itself in material phenomena. In confirmation of this you need only consider the Jesuits' views of natural science, which are strictly materialistic. From their point of view the outer world, the cosmos, is only to be understood in the light of quite materialistic interpretations. In this way, the utmost care has been taken to protect a certain form of faith, which has been cultivated since the Council held in Constantinople in 869—to protect it by keeping external science at the level of materialism. It is true that a kind of smoke-screen has been spread through religion's apparent conflict with materialism even in scientific realms. This however is only apparent, for it does not matter whether one says that there is spirit somewhere, or whether one denies spirit altogether, if the material world itself is not explained spiritually.

You know perhaps that astrophysics represents one of modern science's towering achievements. Its theories set out to study the material starry world, to establish the material unity of the world accessible to the senses. Now one of the greatest astrophysicists is a Roman Jesuit, Father Secchi. There is no difficulty in standing on the ground of modern material science and at the same time adhering to this shade of religious belief. As a matter of fact, a materialistic interpretation of the heavens is nowadays closer to the religious creeds, and especially to one of the Jesuit persuasion, than is spiritual science, for these creeds are particularly concerned *not* to enlighten the world about the relation of matter to spirit. The spiritual is meant to remain an independent form of belief in which nothing is said of a scientific study of the universe; the latter is to remain materialistic, for the moment it ceases to be so it would have to go into what relates to the spiritual—it would have to speak of spirit.

We must take this seriously, otherwise we should overlook the significant fact that Jesuit scientists are the most extreme materialists in the domain of science. They continually allege that man cannot approach the spiritual by researching into nature, and they take trouble to keep the spiritual as far removed as possible from such research. This can be traced even in Father Wasmann's studies of ants.

After these preliminary remarks, let us recall an important fact which apparently unfolds entirely in the spiritual world, but which, when we consider this part of our argument more closely, will make clear to us a parallel phenomenon between spiritual life and the life of the external world of stars. As you know, we divide the post-Atlantean period into epochs of civilization: first the old Indian, second the old Persian, third the Chaldean-Babylonian-Egyptian, fourth the Graeco-Latin; and then there is the fifth, in which we now live, beginning in the middle of the fifteenth century. A sixth will follow this, and so forth. I have frequently shown how the fourth epoch of this ongoing stream of post-Atlantean time began about the year 747 BC, and ceased—roughly speaking about the middle of the fifteenth century—in fact, to be more accurate, it really ended in the year AD 1413. That was the fourth epoch; and we are now in the fifth.

If we thus consider the succession of civilizations, we can describe their characteristics, bearing in mind the descriptions given in *Occult Science*. Thus we can describe the Graeco-Latin, in which the event of Golgotha occurred, but in doing so we need not refer to that event, for we can describe the epoch by connecting it with the preceding one. It is possible to describe the successive epochs in their fundamental nature, and to describe the epoch running from 747 BC to AD 1413 without any historical reference to an important event occurring during this period. Let us recall the time of the occurrence of the event of Golgotha, remembering all we know concerning the civilizations of the most advanced people of the time—the Greek, Roman and Latin. Let us reflect that to these people the event of Golgotha was an unknown affair. It occurred in a small corner of the world, and the first mention of its effects is to be found in Tacitus, the Roman historian, one hundred years later. It was not observed by its contemporaries, least of all by the most cultured.

Thus it becomes clear that there was no intrinsic historical necessity in man's evolution through the first three epochs of civilization, and on into the fourth, that the event of Golgotha should take place. This fact should receive close attention. The event actually took place 747 years after the beginning of the fourth post-Atlantean period. In trying to understand the event of Golgotha, we may say that it gave purpose and meaning to the life of the earth, that the earth would not have had this meaning if evolution had simply gone on as the outcome of the first, second and third post-Atlantean epochs. The event of Golgotha came as an intervention from other worlds. This fact is not sufficiently considered. In modern times several historians have alluded to it, but they have not been able to make anything of it. In fact, history practically omits the event of Golgotha. At most the historians describe the influence of Christianity in the successive post-Christian centuries, but the actual intervention and impulse at work in the Mystery of Golgotha itself is not described in any ordinary description of history. It would indeed be difficult to describe it, if one kept to the ordinary methods of history. Certainly remarkable men—oddly enough, clergy among them—have attempted to explain the causes of the event of Golgotha. Pastor Kalthoff, for instance, and many others. Pastor Kalthoff tried to explain Christianity as a result of people's level of consciousness and economic conditions during the centuries preceding the appearance of Christ. But what did this explanation amount to? In effect it said that people lived in certain economic conditions, and eventually the idea of Christ arose, the dream of Christ, the ideology of Christ as it were; and from these arose Christology. It arose in humanity only as an idea. People like Paul, and a few others, described what had thus arisen as an idea as though it had occurred as a fact in a remote corner of the world! Such explanations mean an abolition of Christianity. It is a noteworthy phenomenon of the nineteenth and beginning of the twentieth centuries that Christian pastors should set themselves the task of saving Christianity by eliminating Christ. People were ashamed to admit the facts of the rise of Christianity outright. They found it more satisfactory to explain the rise of Christology simply as the advent of an idea. Various streams of thought found their way into this domain, and one specialist province of research has very much come to the fore in our times, arising in the materialistic stream of culture which reached its culminating point in Marxism. Thus Kalthoff is a kind of Marxist Pastor who tries to explain Christology through a sort of pious Marxism. Others have ridden other hobby horses in seeking an explanation for the phenomenon of Christianity; why then should not each explain Christianity or explain Christ Jesus, according to his own fancy? A certain psychiatrist explains Christ according to psychiatry, simply by saying that the mighty way in which Christ appeared in his time can be explained today from psychiatry's perspective as due to abnormal consciousness. This is no isolated case. And these are phenomena which must not be disregarded, otherwise we do not see what is happening at the present time, for they are overall symptoms of modern life. We must clearly recognize that what gave the earth its true meaning was an intervention from another world. We must distinguish *two streams in human evolution*, which indeed run side by side today, but only met for the first time at the beginning of our era. One is the Christian stream, which joined the continuous, ongoing current from olden times. Natural science, for instance, has not yet accepted the event of Golgotha and flows on in the continuous evolutionary stream as though that event had never occurred. Spiritual science must endeavour to bring *natural scientific study and Christology* into harmony; for where has Christology any place if the Kant-Laplace theory holds sway and we look back to a primeval mist out of which everything originally formed? Would Christianity ultimately have any real universal significance for man on earth if people regarded the stars as Father Secchi does? He regards the starry heavens materialistically, not as though they gave rise to the event of Golgotha. And that becomes the chief reason for leaving it to *other* authorities to say how man should think of the event of Golgotha. If man can develop no knowledge about this event through his observation and understanding of the world, some other source must be found to tell him what he ought to think of it, and it is obvious that Rome is that source. All these things are so consistently—in a sense, so grandly—thought out, that it is inexcusable to be under any illusions about them at the present difficult and fateful time.

These 747 years occupy a period in the world's evolution of most telling significance, speaking to us of all that is connected with more ancient periods of evolution, all that recalls and is related to past periods of time. A new period begins 747 years after the founding of Rome—which was really founded in 747 BC, not the point of time given in ordinary history books.

Here we have a fresh start therefore; and if we now go back and take the periods of time, we shall have to say that everywhere we must add fresh periods and divisions of time to those already rightly assigned. An entirely new division of the course of time was brought about by the fact that the event of Golgotha fell in this period, as an intervention in human evolution from outside as it were. We must clearly realize the existence of these two streams in world-evolution in so far as man is interwoven with it. If we hold fast to this we can now see something more.

We know that according to the view of ordinary astronomy, the moon moves round the earth. (In reality the moon does not do this as generally described; it too describes a lemniscate; but for the moment we will disregard this.) The moon moves round the earth. While so doing it also rotates around itself. I have already explained this. The moon is a polite lady and always turns the same side to us, her back is always turned away from the earth—though not quite exactly however. To be accurate we ought to say that, *generally speaking*, she always turns the same side to the earth. A seventh part of the concealed side of the moon in fact comes over the edge, as it were, so that really it is not quite always the face of the moon that is turned towards us, for after a time a seventh part comes forwards from behind, and another seventh part retires. This is compensated by the moon's further movements; a whole seventh does not vanish for good, it returns; and the moon reels as she goes round the earth—she actually wobbles and reels. I will only mention this here; in any elementary astronomy book you can look up further details. Could we transport ourselves to a far-distant spot in the cosmos, which according to the calculations of astronomy would be a far-distant star, this rotation of the moon on its own axis would take somewhat more than 27 days. If, however, we transported ourselves to the sun, we would see that the movements of the sun and moon are not uniform, they move with dissimilar velocities; this rotation of the moon seen from the sun would not be the same as seen from a distant star, but would take rather more than 29 days. Thus we may say that the stellar day of the moon is 27 days, and its solar day 29 days.

This of course is connected with all the shifts and transitions which take place in the universe. As we know, the sun rises at a different vernal point every spring, moving round the whole ecliptic, round the whole zodiac in 25,920 years. These reciprocal movements mean that the stellar day of the moon is considerably shorter than its solar day.

Bearing this in mind we may see that this variation is remarkable. Every time we observe the moon's cycle from one full moon to another, we notice a difference between the aspects of sun and moon of almost 2 days. That shows us that we have to do with two movements in cosmic space, which indeed unfold together but do not point back to the same origin. What I have set forth here in terms of the cosmos can be compared with what I have set forth previously from an ethical-spiritual point of view. There is an interval between the beginnings of the individual epochs of civilization in the

one stream and the beginnings of those connected with the
Christ event. When it is full moon, in sidereal time, we still
have to wait for the full moon of solar time. That takes longer
to arrive. There is an interval each time. Thus we have two
currents in the cosmos, two movements, one in which the sun
takes part, and another, the moon; and they are of such nature
that we may say: If we start from the moon-stream, we find the
sun-stream intervening in it, just as the Christ event inter-
venes in the continuous stream of evolution, as though
coming from a quite different world. To the moon-world the
sun-world is a foreign world, from a certain point of view.

Now let us consider this subject once more, from a third
perspective. This we can do by trying to remember exactly
how the human memory works, especially when we include
dreams. We find, for instance, that what has taken place quite
recently, although it does not enter the inner movements and
course of the dream, plays into its picture world. Do not
misunderstand me. We can of course dream of something
that happened to us many years ago, but we do not do so
unless something has recently occurred which is related by
some thought or feeling to earlier years. The whole nature of
dreams is in some way connected with quite recent occurrences. To observe such matters, of course, one needs to be
able to notice the fine details of human life; if such be the case,
observation will furnish as exact results as any exact science.

To what is this due? It is due to the fact that a certain time is
required in order that what we experience in our soul may be
imprinted by the astral body upon the etheric. Approximately
from two and a half to three days, though sometimes after
only one and a half or two days, but never without having slept
upon it, what we have experienced in our intercourse with the
world is imprinted by the astral upon the etheric body. It
always takes a certain time to be established there. Now
compare this fact with another, that is the fact that in everyday
life we repeatedly separate physical body and etheric body

from the astral body and ego in sleep, and in waking unite them. We may therefore say that between birth and death there is a somewhat tenuous connection between the physical and etheric bodies on the one hand, and the ego and astral body on the other. For the physical and etheric bodies *always* remain together between birth and death, and the astral body and ego remain together also, but not the astral and etheric bodies; every night they separate. There is thus a looser connection between the astral and etheric bodies than between the etheric and physical; and this is again expressed in the fact that there must in a sense be a certain parting of the astral and etheric bodies before what we have experienced in the astral body is imprinted upon the etheric body. When some event influences us, it does so of course in the waking condition. This means it works upon the physical, etheric and astral bodies and the ego. There is, however, a difference in their reception of its effect. The astral body takes it up at once. The etheric needs a certain time for the impression to be so established that complete harmony arises between the astral and etheric. Does this not clearly and distinctly show that although all four bodies or principles of the human being experience each event or occurrence that affect us there are two currents in us which do not run the same course in relation to the outer world, one stream needing longer than the other? There we have the same as we have in history, the same too as we have in the cosmos—moon and sun, primal pagan evolution and Christianity; and now, etheric and astral. Always a differentiation or interval in time. Thus we find this interaction of two streams appearing in our ordinary life, two streams which come together and combine in our lives, yet cannot be grasped so simply as to permit the causes and effects of one stream to wholly coincide with the causes and effects of the other.

These things are of fundamental importance for our consideration of the universe and life, and cannot be dispensed with if one wishes to understand the world. There are other facts too which people also entirely overlook nowadays. And what do all these things show? They indicate the existence of a certain harmony between cosmic life, history and the life of individual human beings; but a harmony not constructed as is usual today in people's efforts to account for everything through biological and genetic perspectives of a quite materialistic kind. The consequence is that we cannot make do with a single kind of astronomy but need different astronomies, one of the sun, another of the moon. If we have two clocks, one always a little slower than the other, then the latter will always be ahead; but we should never assume that the cause of the one lies in the other. That would be impossible. So too, although there is a certain regularity and lawfulness in the one being always the same amount behind the other, the two streams of which we have been speaking have nothing to do with one another; they only work together through the fact that I observe them together. Solar astronomy has nothing to do with lunar astronomy, though the two work side by side in our universe.

It is important to bear this in mind; and just as we have to distinguish between solar and lunar astronomy in relation to the movements of sun and moon, so too must we distinguish in history between what takes place in us through succeeding periods of civilization, and what takes place in us through the cycles of time whose central point is the event of Golgotha. These two things work together in the world, but if we wish to grasp them, we must discriminate between them. We see the prototype of historical time in the cosmos, and we see the ultimate expression—I do not say the effect—but the last expression of these universal facts in our own life in the two or three days which must elapse before our thoughts have become so 'firm' that they no longer remain above in the astral body where they may appear as dreams, as it were, of themselves, but descend into the etheric body and must be recaptured by our own active memory or by something that reminds us of them. Within us, therefore, one movement flows into the other. Just as we have to realize that there is a lunar current which, as it were, generates independent systems or structures of movement, so we must realize that in our human constitution our physical and etheric bodies are more closely connected with one aspect of the macrocosm, while our astral body and ego, in contrast, are more closely related to a different aspect of the macrocosm.

Modern science casts a veil of darkness over such things that confuses everything, positing a cosmic mist which forms into a ball from which the sun, moon and planets emerge. This is not the case: the sun and moon are not of the same origin but are two streams running side by side; and just as little can man's human ego and astral body be traced to the same origin as his physical and etheric bodies. They are two different streams. In the book *Occult Science* you can find that these two streams must be traced back to the Sun stage of evolution. Then to be sure, on going back from the Sun to the Saturn stage, one comes to a sort of unity. This, however, lies very far back indeed; from the Sun stage onwards, there is a continual tendency for two streams to emerge and run side by side.

In this account I wished to show how necessary it is to throw light on the parallel between cosmic existence, history and human existence, in order to arrive at a view of man's relationship to cosmic movements. We have seen that a proper understanding will lead not to *one* astronomy, but *two*: a *solar* and a *lunar* astronomy. Similarly there is non-Christian evolution—our natural science is still heathen—and Christian evolution. In our day many people try to prevent these two streams, which have met on earth in order to work together, from their proper confluence.

Consider for instance, how the whole drift of a book such as that by Traub*—the rest of the book has no meaning without this—consists in the claim: 'Yes, Dr Steiner wishes to unite the two streams, heathen and Christian. We will not let that happen. We want natural science to remain heathen, so that there may be no need to bring about anything in Christendom which may reconcile it with natural science.' Of course, if science is allowed to be heathen, Christianity cannot unite with it. Then people can continue to say: 'science is carried on externally, materialistically; Christendom is founded on faith. The two must not be reconciled.' Christ, however, truly did not appear on earth in order that the heathen impulse should increase in power, separate from and alongside his impulse; he came to permeate the heathen impulse. The task of the present time is to unite what man would keep asunder— knowledge and faith—and this must come to pass. Therefore attention must be drawn to such things as I indicated in one of my recent public lectures. On the one hand the Church has decided that cosmology should have no place in Christology; and on the other hand cosmology is now based on the principle of the indestructibility of matter and force.[†] But if matter and force are regarded as indestructible and eternal, this leads to a trampling under foot of all ideals. And then Christianity too is meaningless. Only when what constitutes matter and its laws is regarded as a transitory phenomenon, and when the Christ impulse becomes a seed of what will exist when matter and force no longer hold sway as they do now, but have died away, only then will Christianity, ethical ideals and human worth have a true meaning. There are two great antitheses: the one arising from the final logical conclusion of heathenism— 'Matter and force are eternal ', and the other arising from

---

* *Rudolf Steiner als Philosoph und Theosoph* ('Rudolf Steiner as philosopher and theosophist'), by Friedrich Traub. Tubingen, 1919.
[†] The word 'force' on this page is generally rendered 'energy' in English scientific writing (Indestructibility of Matter and Energy).

Christianity—'Heaven and earth shall pass away, but my words shall not pass away.'

These are the two greatest contrasts of outlook which can be expressed, and our age urgently needs not to be confused about such things, but with wakeful mind to look earnestly towards a right understanding of the world, in which moral human value and the Christian impulse in world evolution are not overwhelmed by the illusion of indestructible matter and indestructible force. More of this in the next lecture.

Lecture 13

I have now brought together many and various matters which may help us gain a sense of the structure of the universe in its relation to man. We have seen—and this must be emphasized again and again—that the universe cannot be understood without man. In other words we cannot understand the universe in itself without relating it to man and vice versa. If one wishes to form a simple, clear idea of man's connection with the universe, one need only think of a theme in elementary astronomy—the so-called 'obliquity of the ecliptic'—that is, the oblique position of the earth's axis in relation to the line, the curve, which passes through the zodiac. This obliquity of the ecliptic may be understood and even interpreted as you will; we are not for the moment concerned with whether it accords with reality or not but rather with bringing a certain fact to your notice. If the earth's axis—the axis on which the earth turns daily—were perpendicular to the plane through the zodiacal ecliptic, then day and night would be equal throughout the year over the whole earth. If the earth's axis lay *in* the ecliptic, then over the whole earth one half of the year would be day and one half night. Both these extremes do in a certain respect actually occur at the equator and at the poles. But in between lie regions where the length of day varies through the year. We need only reflect a little on this matter to arrive at the tremendous significance for the whole evolution of earthly civilization, of the position of the earth's axis in space. All of us throughout the globe would be Eskimos if the axis lay in the ecliptic; and if it were vertical to the ecliptic, the whole earth would be filled with the kind of civilization that prevails at the equator.

Of course an understanding of the truth depends upon what interpretation we give it, but *any* interpretation of this position of the earth's axis will serve to make one perceive the connection between man, his culture and civilization, and the structure of the universe. However we interpret this fact, it compels us to regard man and the earth as a unity, at least as far as his physical being is concerned, not as an independent and separate entity. As physical being, man is not a separate entity but is part of the whole earth, just as a hand severed from the human organism cannot be regarded as having a separate existence in any true sense. It dies; it can only be imagined in connection with the organism. A rose dies when plucked, and as a reality it is only conceivable in connection with the rose bush which is rooted in the earth; so too, to understand man in his entirety, in his totality, one cannot regard him as simply enclosed in the boundaries of his skin.

Thus what we experience on earth must be considered in connection with the earth's axis. It is important in a world view based on reality that what is a partial truth should not be interpreted as the whole truth. To approach the totality of man as a being of soul and spirit we need to understand that his physical nature is not a self-contained, separate reality. As a being of soul and spirit, the human being is a complete and self-contained individual entity. What he inhabits between birth and death however—the physical and etheric bodies— are not separate realities in themselves, they are part of the whole earth, and as we shall presently see, they are even part of another whole.

This brings us to something which must be observed still more closely, which I keep returning to again and again. The ideas we form of man almost always tend, unconsciously, to our regarding him as a kind of solid body. True, we are aware that he is not precisely a hard body, that he is to some extent plastic, but we are very often unaware that he consists of 75% or more fluid, and that only the residue can be regarded as a solid mineral being. Man is really 75% a water being. Now I ask you, therefore, is it possible to describe the human organism, as is usually done, in sharp outlines—saying 'Here we have the lobes of the brain, here this organ,' and so forth, and then assume that the solidly circumscribed organs combine in their activity to bring about the activity of the whole organism? There is no sense whatever in that. Instead we should bear in mind the fact that, within the limits of our skin, we are more like a sea in flux and movement; that what is purely inwardly surging fluidity in us therefore also has a meaning, and that we should not describe man as if he were more or less a solid body. In spiritual science this has very deep significance. For precisely when we consider the *solid* in man, which is in a certain way related to what is the external mineral world, we find that what is solid in the human being has a certain relation to the earth.

We have observed all sorts of connection and correspondence between man and the world around him; and now we will examine the relation of his solid substance to the earth. This connection exists; the *watery* element in man has, however, no primary connection with the earth but with the planetary universe beyond, and especially with the *moon*. Precisely as the moon, not directly but indirectly, has a relation to the ebb and flow of the tides, to certain configurations of the earth's fluid element, so too it has a connection with what takes place in the fluid part of the human organism. Yesterday I described two kinds of astronomy—the first of which applies to the sun, and also to the earth. We ourselves are part of that astronomy inasmuch as our organisms contain solid substances. Lunar astronomy, however, is different. We are affected by lunar astronomy in so far as it is connected with what is fluid within us. Thus we see that the forces of the cosmos work into both solid and fluid aspects of our physical nature.

The far greater significance of this, though, is that what we call our ego has a direct influence on what is solid in us and that what we call our astral body has an *indirect* influence on our fluid element—so that what works from the soul and spirit upon our organization comes also into connection with all the forces of the cosmos via our physical body. Throughout history people have always observed these movements of the cosmos from the most varied points of view. When we look back to the ancient Persian civilization we find that people were already researching into the movements of the universe. The Chaldeans did this too, and the Egyptians, and it is not without interest to study the Egyptians' approach to the movements of the universe. Of course there were apparently quite material reasons for the Egyptians to study the connection between earth and outer cosmos, for their land depended upon the inundations of the Nile which took place precisely when the sun was in a definite position in the universe. This position could be determined by that of Sirius; so that the Egyptians had come to make observations about the position of the sun in relation to what we now call the fixed stars. The Egyptian priests especially, in their Mysteries, undertook extensive researches into the relation of the sun to the other stars. As I have already said, the Egyptians knew perfectly well that each year the sun appeared to have shifted its position in the heavens in regard to the other stars; and they used this fact to calculate that the stars—whether apparently or really is immaterial just now—had a certain velocity in their daily course around the heavens, and that the daily movement of the sun also had a certain velocity, but not quite so great as that of the stars. The sun always lagged somewhat behind. The Egyptians knew and recorded the fact that the sun lagged behind the stars by about one day in 72 years; so that when a particular star which rose with the sun in a particular year rises again 72 years later, the sun does not rise with it but 24 hours later. A star belonging to the world of fixed stars, a star in the zodiac, outstrips the sun by one day, one full day, in every 72 years. Multiply 72 by 360 and we obtain 25,920 years. That is a number which we often meet with. It is the time the sun takes, as it increasingly lags behind, to get back to its starting-point, having thus gone round the whole zodiac. Every 72 years, therefore, the sun falls behind by exactly one degree, for a circle has, as we know, 360 degrees. According to this reckoning, the Egyptians divided the great cosmic year— which really comprises 25,920 years—into 360 'days'; but such a day was 72 years long. And 72 years, what is that? It is the average span of a human life. Certainly there are individuals who live to be older, others not so old, but it is the average length of a human life. Thus one can say that the universe is so constructed that it sustains each human life for a solar day, which is 72 years. True, we are emancipated from that. We can be born at any time; but as physical human beings between birth and death our life here is governed by the solar day. Referring to historical records, one generally finds that the ordinary year of the Egyptians was reckoned as 360 days (not 365¼ as it actually is), until later on this was found to be at odds with the course of the stars, and the other five days had to be inserted. How did it come about that the Egyptians originally took 360 days for the year? In the cosmic year a degree—that is, a 360th part—is actually a cosmic day of 72 years. Thus in the Egyptian Mysteries it was taught that man is so connected with the cosmos, that the duration of his life is one day of the cosmic year. He was thus integrated into the cosmos. His relation to the cosmos was made clear to him.

But through circumstances which belong to the decadence of the whole evolution of the Egyptian people, the essential nature of man and his connection with the cosmos was *not* then made known to the wide mass of the Egyptians—that is characteristic of those times. It was said that if all people knew the nature of their being, how it is integrated into the cosmos, and that the duration of their own life is subsumed in the duration of the sun's revolution, then they would not allow themselves to be ruled, for each would regard himself as a member of the universe. Only those were allowed to know this who it was believed were called to be leaders. The rest were not to possess such knowledge of the cosmos, but a knowledge of daily things only. This is connected with the decadence of the Egyptian civilization. And while it was right, in respect to many other things, that people not ready for this should not be initiated into the Mysteries, this was extended for the sole purpose of giving power to the leaders and rulers.

Now a great deal of what permeates our human souls today has originally come from oriental sources. Traditional Christianity too contains much that has come from oriental sources; but Roman Christianity, especially, was influenced by a strong impulse that came from Egypt. Just as the Egyptians were kept in ignorance about their real connection with the cosmos, so in certain circles of Romanism the view prevails that people must be kept in ignorance of their connection with the cosmos as it was brought about through the Mystery of Golgotha. Hence the fierce conflict which arises when, from the inner needs of our age, we emphasize that the event of Golgotha is not simply something which must be regarded as unrelated to the rest of our outlook but that it must rather be integrated into it; when we show how what took place on Golgotha is really connected with the whole universe and its constitution. It is therefore regarded as the worst heresy to describe Christ as the sun spirit, as we have done.

It must not be supposed that the point at issue is not well known to people in high places who do their utmost to combat what I have just said. They are fully aware of such things. But just as the Egyptian priest knew quite well that the ordinary year does not have 360 days but 365¼, so certain people are perfectly well aware that the matter with which the Christ Mystery deals is also connected with the sun Mysteries. But present-day humanity is to be hindered from receiving this *knowledge*, the very knowledge that it needs; for as I have already said, such circles much prefer a materialistic view of the universe to spiritual science. Materialistic science also has its practical consequences, in which again the present time may be compared with ancient Egypt. As I have said, the Egyptians were dependent upon the course of the sun, in other words on the relation of the earthly to the heavenly, as regards their external civilization. Withholding knowledge of the connection of cosmic phenomena and their effect on the cultivation of the land represented a certain power in the hands of the declining priesthood, for thereby the Egyptian labourers had to submit to direction from the priests, who had the requisite knowledge.

Now if the European and American civilizations were to retain their present character, adhering only to the materialistic, Copernican view of the universe—with its off-shoot, the Kant-Laplace theory—a materialistic outlook would necessarily arise to explain earthly phenomena, biological, physical and chemical. It would be impossible for this kind of materialistic outlook to include a moral world order. It could not embrace the Christ event, for it is impossible to be a believer in the materialistic view of the world and at the same time a Christian; that is an inner lie, it is something that *cannot* be, if one is honest and upright. Hence it was inevitable that the practical consequences should be seen in Europe and American culture of the split between materialism on the one hand and a moral world view, creed and faith on the other, which has no relation to a materialistic outlook. The consequence of this was that those who had no outward reason for being inwardly dishonest threw faith overboard, and made the materialistic world view the basis for human life also. Thus the materialistic world view also became one which governed society. The further consequence of this for our European and American civilization would be that man's view of things would become purely materialistic—he would know nothing of the earth's connection with cosmic powers, in the sense that we have described it. Within certain elite circles, however, *knowledge* of the connection with the cosmos would remain, just as the Egyptian priests kept the knowledge of the Platonic year, the great cosmic year and the great cosmic day; and such circles could hope then to rule the people who under materialism degenerate into barbarism.

Of course these things have been said today only from a sense of duty towards truth; but such a duty to truth demands that they be said. It is important that a certain number of people should realize how necessary it is to give the Mystery of Golgotha its cosmological significance. This significance must be recognized by a number of people, who for their part undertake a certain responsibility that the fact should not remain hidden from earthly humanity—the fact that humanity is connected with the super-earthly Spirit, who lived in Palestine in the man Jesus, at the beginning of our era. It is necessary that knowledge should not be withheld of the entrance of Christ from the super-earthly world into the man Jesus of Nazareth. Such knowledge and understanding is implicit in overcoming that dishonesty which is so general today in questions of world view and religious faith. For what do people do nowadays? We are told on the one hand that the earth moves in an ellipse round the sun and has evolved as the Kant-Laplace theory explains, and we subscribe to this; and on the other hand we are told that at the beginning of our era such and such events took place in Palestine. These two things are accepted, without being connected; people accept them and think it of no consequence. It is not without consequence, however, for it is much less evil when we are conscious of such a lie and discrepancy than when it takes shape unconsciously, and degrades us and drags us down. For if we consider a lie as it appears in a person's conscious awareness, every time he falls asleep it leaves his physical and etheric bodies with his consciousness, and lives on in spaceless, timeless being, in eternal being, while the person is in dreamless sleep. There is prepared all which can result from the lie in the future; that is, everything is made ready to correct it, if it is in our consciousness. But if the lie is unconscious, it remains with our physical and etheric bodies lying in bed. When we do not occupy these bodies, it then belongs to the cosmos, and not to the earthly cosmos alone, but to the whole cosmos; there it works for the destruction of the cosmos; above all, for the destruction of the whole of humanity, for this destruction *begins* in humanity itself.

Man can escape what threatens humanity in this way by no other means than by striving after inner truth in relation to these supreme questions of existence. Thus the impulses of our time are in a sense calling on humanity today to realize that a materialistic astronomy should no longer exist which knows nothing of how the event of Golgotha took shape at a particular point in time. Every astronomy that includes the moon in the structure of the universe in just the same way as it does the sun and earth, instead of allowing the two streams to run into one another, but still as separate streams—every such astronomy is no Christian astronomy but a heathen one. Therefore a Christian perspective must reject every theory of evolution which describes the universe homogeneously. If you follow my book *Occult Science*, you will see how, in the description of the Saturn and Sun periods of evolution, the stream divides into two, which then intermingle and work together. Here we have two streams. In the descriptions usually given, however, the ideas presented accord wholly with the non-Christian, heathen stream, right down to the smallest details. You know that Darwinian theorists describing the evolution of organic form would say that first there were simple organic forms, then more complicated forms, then more and more complicated forms, and so forth, until man evolved. But this is not so. If we take man as threefold, his head alone has evolved from a lower animal form. What is joined to it has arisen later. Thus we cannot say that in our vertebral column we have something which transforms itself into head, but we must see things as follows. Our head certainly arose from earlier structures which were spine-like; but the *present* spine has nothing to do with that sequence of evolution, it is a later appendage. What is now our head-organization has arisen from a differently formed spine.

This I say for those who are interested in the theory of descent. I mention it so that you may see that a straight line leads from cosmic considerations to consideration of what lies in human evolution, and so that you may see the necessity for an enlightened spiritual science in all the different realms of knowledge and life. For science must not simply continue to develop, as did the science of the last century, under the influence of the materialistic view of the universe, which is itself the offspring of a materialistic comprehension of Christianity. We owe materialism to the materialization of the Christian view of the universe. Teaching of the cosmic Christ must be re-established in opposition to the materialized form of Christianity we have today. This is the most important task of our time; and until its importance is realized, man will not be able to see clearly in any domain.

I wanted to tell you these things, because they will enable you to understand better why ill-willed opponents fight so strenuously against what we are nowadays presenting to the world. I was obliged to connect this whole study with a kind of cosmology, consideration of which we will continue in the next lecture.

Lecture 14

My chief aim in what follows is to show how the two streams of world history, the heathen or pagan stream and the Christian stream, meet in our life, how they affect one another and are connected with events in the whole universe. In order to examine this more closely, however, we must today first engage in some preliminary observations. It is essential that we should discriminate as exactly as possible how the pagan world view, taking it in the widest sense (for indeed, it is still and must remain at the basis of our modern outlook)—how this pagan world view differs from the Christian, whose full reality has so far passed into human awareness only to a very limited extent. The point is, as I have often pointed out, that we have now come to a time when what we may call the scientific picture of the world and what we call the moral order of the universe—to which of course, also belongs the religious view of the world—stand side by side, utterly unconnected. For people today, more than they are aware of, science and morality are two quite separate things, which if they honestly strive to understand the world through modern science they cannot begin to unite. That is why the greatest part of the progressive theology of the nineteenth and twentieth centuries actually contains no Christology. I have often remarked on the existence of such books as Adolf Harnack's *The Nature of Christianity*, in which there is no reason whatever why the name of Christ should be mentioned; for what is referred to there as 'Christ' is none other than the deity met with in the Old Testament as Jehovah. There is really no actual difference between Harnack's 'Christ' and Jehovah—

that is, there is no difference between what is said of the Christ Being and what followers of the Old Testament view of the universe said of their God Jehovah. If we take the idea of Christ held today by many people and compare it with the rest of their outlook on life, there is no reason whatever why they should speak of Christ and Christianity; for to speak of Christ and Christianity and at the same time hold the kind of nationalist views they do is an absolute contradiction. These things only escape people's notice today because they avoid courageously drawing the logical conclusion from what is there before them. The widest rift, however, the widest gulf, exists between the view of things held by natural science and that held by Christianity; and the most important task of our time is to build a bridge over the gulf. A scientific outlook, such as every farm labourer has today—even if he is unaware of it—is an offspring of the nineteenth century; and it is good not always to describe these things in the abstract, but to see how they also become concrete and specific.

I have often mentioned the name of a prominent personality of the nineteenth century, one who directs our attention directly to the scientific world view—I refer to Julius Robert Mayer, whom we must associate with the nineteenth-century scientific outlook although in his case it is somewhat misleading. You know that it is popularly believed that the law of conservation of energy originated with him—or, to speak more accurately, the law that the universe contains a constant sum of forces which can be neither increased nor lessened, and can only be changed into one another. Heat, mechanical force, electricity, chemical energy, all change one into the other, yet the quantity of energy existing in the universe always remains the same. Every modern physicist holds this view. Although people are not particularly aware of this law of the conservation of energy as they go about their lives, they think of natural phenomena in a way that can only be thought of when one is influenced by this law. You see, it is important to realize that certain principles may affect our actions, even when such principles remain unconscious. Suppose, for instance, that one wished to make a dog understand that a double quantity of meat means that a single quantity has been consumed twice; it could not be done. The dog could not take that in consciously, but *practically* he will *act* according to this principle; for if he has the chance of snapping at a small piece or at one twice the size, he will as a rule, seize the larger, other conditions being equal. And likewise a human being can be influenced by a principle without explaining it to himself in abstract form as such. Thus most people do not think of the law of conservation of energy, but they do picture the whole of nature in a way that accords with this law, because what they were taught in school was taught on the assumption that the law of conservation of energy exists. It is interesting to see how Mayer's line of thought expressed itself when he had to put it clearly to others who did not as yet think along the same lines.

Julius Robert Mayer had a friend who kept a record of many of their conversations. He relates many interesting facts, which enable one to gain a full understanding of the nineteenth-century mode of thought. Let me characterize this in the following way by means of something quite external. Julius Robert Mayer was so thoroughly steeped in the whole mode of ideas leading to that of the conservation of energy, of the mere transmutation of one force into another, that as a rule whenever he met a friend in the street he could not help calling to him from a distance: 'Nothing comes of nothing!' Visiting his friend one day—Rümelin was the friend's name— knocking at the door and opening it, these were his first words, even before greeting his friend: 'Nothing comes of nothing.' So deeply was this saying rooted in Mayer's consciousness.

Rümelin tells of a very interesting discussion in which he, not as yet knowing very much of the law of the conservation of energy, wished to have it explained. Julius Robert Mayer, who came from Heilbronn (where you can see his monument) said: 'If two horses are drawing a carriage and they go for some distance, what will happen?'—'Well,' said Rümelin, 'the travellers in the carriage will arrive at Ohringen.'—'But if they turn and go back without having done anything in Ohringen, and return to Heilbronn?' 'Well,' replied Rümelin, 'in that case the one journey has so to speak cancelled the other, so that there is apparently no result; yet in actual fact the travellers came and went between Heilbronn and Ohringen.' 'No,' said Mayer, 'that is only a secondary effect; it has nothing to do with what actually happened. The outcome of the expenditure of energy on the part of the horses is something quite different. Through this expenditure of energy the horses themselves first grew hotter, secondly the axles of the carriage round which the wheels moved became hotter, and thirdly if we were to gauge with a delicate thermometer the grooves made by the wheels in the road, we should find that the warmth within them was greater than at the sides. That is the actual result. In the horses themselves, substances were also consumed through metabolism. All this is the actual effect. The other effect, that the people travelled backwards and forwards between Heilbronn and Ohringen, is a secondary effect, but not the actual physical occurrence. The actual physical occurrence was the energy used by the horses, the transmutation into increased heat in the horses, the increased heat in the axles, the consumption of cart-grease through friction in the wheels, the warming of the tracks on the road, and so forth.' When one measures—as Mayer then did and specified the corresponding amount—one finds that the whole of the energy which the horses exerted passed into these forms of heat. The rest is all a secondary matter, a side-issue.

This has of course a certain influence on the way we view things, and the ultimate result is that we must say: 'Well, we must free natural phenomena from everything that is a side-issue in the sense of strict scientific thought, for side-issues have nothing to do with scientific thought in the sense it is understood in the nineteenth century. The secondary effect is quite outside the bounds of what natural science examines.' If, however, we ask: How does what we may call moral law come to expression? In what are human worth and human dignity expressed? Certainly not in the 'primary' fact that the energy of the horses is transmuted into the heat of the carriage axles! Let us reflect, however, how natural science gives no consideration whatever to this secondary effect. People of the nineteenth century, and even Kant in the eighteenth, formed their view of the origin of the universe simply on the basis of principles which Julius Robert Mayer so sharply defined, when he separated out what belongs to nature alone from all that was for him merely secondary effect.

If we bear this clearly in mind, we are obliged to recognize that people had to view the universe as constructed on the principle of natural law; all that took place through Christianity, for instance, becomes nothing more than a secondary effect, like the fact of the people journeying by coach from Heilbronn to Ohringen—for what these people actually did there has no relevance for natural science. Yet, do these two streams not cross in some way or other?

Let us suppose Rümelin had not been quite satisfied by this explanation, but had raised the following objection—I know it does not hold good for the physicist of today, but it is applicable to the construction of a general view of the universe—suppose the following was said: If the people who were travelling from Heilbronn to Ohringen had *chosen* not to do so, the horses would not have expended their energy, the transmutation into heat would not have taken place, or it would have happened at a different place and under different conditions. Thus in our scientific consideration of what happened we are limited to that part of the event which does not lead us back to the ultimate cause. The event *would never have taken place* if the travellers had not supposed they had something to do in Ohringen. Thus what natural science must regard as a side-issue nevertheless affects natural occurrences. Or, suppose that the travellers had something to do in Ohringen at a definite hour. Suppose the carriage axles not only became hot, but that one of them broke—in that case they could not have continued their journey. The breaking of the axle would then of course be explicable scientifically, but what occurred through this natural phenomenon—namely, that something planned could not be carried out—might, as can easily be imagined, have tremendously far-reaching consequences, leading moreover to other natural processes, which would in their turn have led to further consequences.

Thus we see that even when one stays put in the purely logical realm of cause and effect very significant and grave questions arise. We must at once say that these cannot be answered by the world view which people assimilate through education; they cannot be answered without spiritual science. They simply cannot be answered without it; for before the tendency to the natural-scientific mode of thought arose, which was first brought to such precision by Julius Robert Mayer, there was not that sharp line of division between the natural-scientific mode of thought and moral thought. If we consider the twelfth or thirteenth century, we find that people's views of the moral order and the physical order always harmonized. Today people no longer read seriously; but if you read such works—I might say, there are not many things left from olden times which have come down to our days quite unadulterated—but if you take works which are like vestiges of ancient world views, you will discover many things that prove how in earlier times the moral was carried into the physical, and the physical raised to the moral. Read one of these—now already somewhat adulterated yet still fairly readable—read one of the writings of Basilius Valentinus.

When you read there about metals, planets, medicinal drugs, in almost every line you will come across adjectives applied to the metals—good, bad, sagacious metals, and the like; which show that moral thinking was even applied to this domain. That of course could not be done today. Abstraction has gone so far that natural phenomena have been severed from all the secondary effects, as we may see in Julius Robert Mayer; one cannot say that it was through the kindness of the horses' feet that the axle-grease used up the warmth produced by their movement! It is not possible to introduce any moral aspect into this scientific context. There are two domains, the natural and the moral, and these stand quite separately alongside one another. But if the world really worked in the way such concepts conceive, man could not exist at all in our world, he would not be there—for what is the reason for the present physical form of man?

When I speak here of man's physical form, I must ask you to take the word 'form' seriously. The natural philosophers of today do not take the expression 'human form' seriously. What do they do? Like Huxley and others, they count the bones of man and of the higher animals, and from the number of these they draw the conclusion that man is only a more highly evolved stage of the animal. Or they count the muscles and so forth. We have repeatedly had cause to show the essential point: that the line of the animal spine is horizontal, while the human spine is vertical; and although certain animals raise themselves, the erect position is not character-istic for them. What is characteristic of the animal is the horizontal line of the spine. Upon this depends the animal's whole form. Thus I ask you to take seriously what I wish to express by the word 'form'.

This *form* of man, where must we look spiritually for its origin, its primary physical origin in the universe? I have already touched on this point in these lectures, I have pointed to the starry heavens which move—whether apparently or actually is immaterial at the moment—round the earth; the sun also. Thus the sun follows the same path. But if we take into consideration the fact that the sun shifts its rising point each spring, falling behind a little in relation to the stars, we come to a specially important fact. The change in position of the vernal point can be seen in the fact that the constellation in the following year rises earlier than the sun and sets earlier, showing us that the sun falls behind. I have pointed out that even the ancient Egyptians knew that if the circumference of the heavens is divided into 360 degrees, the sun falls one day behind in 72 years. That is, in 360 times 72 years, or 25,920 years, it falls back through the whole circle and returns to the star from which it started 25,920 years before.

Thus we have the fact that in the universe both the stars and the sun circulate in this way—I will not go into the question of whether this revolution is only apparent or not, the important point under consideration is that the sun travels more slowly, falling behind one degree of the cosmic circle in 72 years; and 72 years, as I have already indicated, is the normal duration of a person's life. Man lives 72 years, exactly the period the sun takes to fall one degree behind the other stars.

We have lost the right feeling for these things. Even as late as the Hebraic Mysteries, the teacher still impressed very strongly upon his scholars that it is Jehovah who causes the sun to linger behind the stars and, with the force which the sun thus retained, he fashioned the human form, which is his earthly image. Thus, mark well, the stars run their course quickly, the sun more slowly, and so a slight difference arises which, according to these ancient Mysteries, was what produced the human form. Man is born out of time, in such a way that he owes his existence to the difference in velocity between the cosmic day of the stars and the cosmic day of the sun. Nowadays we could put it like this: If the sun were not in the universe as it is, if it were just a star like other stars, having the same velocity as other stars, what would be the consequence? The consequence would be that luciferic powers alone would rule. That this is not so, that man is able to withdraw his whole being from luciferic powers, is due to the circumstance that the sun does not share in the velocity of the stars but lags behind them, not developing luciferic velocity but the velocity of Jehovah. And on the other hand, if there were only the sun velocity and not that of the stars, man would not be able to project his mental powers ahead of the rest of his development powers, as he does at present. Such a condition would not fit well with man's overall evolution. In our time this is very striking. If we have studied spiritual science seriously, we know that someone of 36, for instance, understands things he could not at 25. Experience is necessary for the comprehension of certain things. This is not widely acknowledged today, for someone of 25 feels himself complete. He is only complete as regards mental powers, but not in experience, for experience is gained more slowly than understanding. If this were taken into account, we should not find that the young people of today already viewed things from a fixed perspective, for they would know that they could not do so before acquiring a certain amount of experience. Understanding travels with the stars, experience with the sun. Taking the span of a human life to be 72 years, we say that it lasts the time the sun takes to retrograde one degree. Why is this? The reason lies in a certain delicate adjustment in the cosmos. Our preliminary study obliges me to ask you to follow me for a little while into this domain.

If we consider a lunar eclipse occurring in a certain year, then there will be a certain date when the eclipse can occur. The lunar eclipse occurs on the same date about every 18 years, and in the same constellation. There is a periodical rhythm in lunar eclipses, a rhythm of 18 years. That is just a quarter of a cosmic day and just a quarter of a human life. Man, if I may so express it, endures four such periods of darkness. Why? Because in the universe everything is in numerical harmony. On average, man's rhythmic activity of his heart gives him not only 72 years of life, but 72 pulse beats, and approximately 18 respirations—again the quarter—per minute. This numerical accord is expressed in the universe by the rhythm between the 18 years—the Chaldean Saros period, so-called because the Chaldeans first discovered it—and the solar period; and it is the same rhythm as is also to be found in man in the inner mobility between his respiration and his pulse beats. Plato said, not without reason: 'God geometrizes, arithmetizes.' Thus our 72 years of life, co-ordinated also with our heart and pulse activity in which the pulse is four times faster than the breathing, goes through the Saros period four times. Each life span is therefore marked by four such 'pulses'. Our whole human organism is constructed in relation to the universe, but we only see into its significance when we bear something else in mind as well.

As I said in one of the foregoing lectures, we only properly gauge the movement of the moon, its rotation round its axis, when we connect its revolution not with the solar but with the stellar day. If we have stellar time in view, we must consider a shorter time, 27½ days for the revolution of the moon. I have told you that the moon's revolution does not quite accord with that of the sun, but with the time of the stars. Hence we only understand our lunar movement aright when we do not think of it as belonging to the solar movement, but to that of the stars. In a certain sense therefore, the solar movement is outside the system to which the moon and stars belong. Thus our place in the universe relates on the one hand to the stellar-lunar system, and on the other to solar movement.

Here we see the gradual divergence of solar and stellar astronomy. As we have seen, one astronomy alone confuses everything. We can only reach a right understanding if, not limited to *one* astronomy, we say: On the one hand we have the starry system which, in a certain respect, contains the moon; and on the other, the system to which the sun belongs.

They mutually interpenetrate. They work together. But we are wrong if we apply the same law to the two.

When we realize that we have two quite different astronomies, we can also see that the cosmos in which we are embedded has two origins, but we are so placed that these two streams flow together in us. They fuse in us human beings. What is it then that takes place in us? Suppose that only what science acknowledges took place in us—all sorts of things would take place in the human organism, movements of substances and so forth; these would extend over the whole organism, also to the brain and consequently to the senses. What then would the consequence be if the whole transmutation of substances which goes on in the human organism and which is part of the cosmos as I have explained—if this metabolism were to extend to the *brain*? We should never be able to have an awareness of our own thinking capacity. Oxygen, iron and other substances, carbon and so forth—of these we should say, in their mutual relations, '*they* think in us'. But as a matter of fact we are not conscious of any such thing. There is no question of its being in our consciousness. What we have as a fact of consciousness is the content of our soul-life. This can only exist by virtue of the fact that this quite material process breaks down and destroys itself, and that in us there actually is no conservation of energy and substance, but room is made by the annihilation of substance for the development of our thought-life. In fact, man is the one arena in which an actual *annihilation of substance* takes place. We shall never realize this as long as we do not properly understand man as such, but are only conscious of what is not human.

Now, if we start from the fact that after 72 years the sun falls one degree behind in the celestial sphere, that there is this difference of velocity between the movement of the stars and that of the sun (a difference which works in us, converges, as it were, in us); and if we then picture to ourselves how the formation of our head comes from the starry heavens, and how when we, according to a very beautiful saying, first 'see the light' we become involved in the sun's movement, then we must say: There is in us a continual tendency to oppose the more rapid velocity of the stars with a lesser velocity. There is opposition to what the stars do within us. What is the effect of this opposition? It is the destruction of what the stars bring about in us materially, its destruction. Destruction of the purely material law thus comes about through solar activity. Hence we may say that if, in our progress through the world as human beings, we kept pace, as it were, with the stars, we should accompany them in such a way as to be subject to the material laws of the universe. But this we are not. The solar laws oppose it, they hold us back. There is something within us which holds things back. One can calculate this—though the calculation cannot be pursued here, first because it would take too long and secondly because you would not be able to follow it. Here, let us say, a certain movement occurs at a certain speed (arrow pointing downwards), i.e. a flow takes place with a certain velocity; and the stream then fuses with another stream—it must be assumed that the other flow is going not in the same but in the opposite direction (arrow upwards). The two streams therefore flow into one another. Or imagine a wind whirling with a certain velocity from above downwards, and another from below upwards, and they whirl

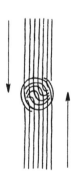

into one another. If we take the difference of velocity between the downward and the upward current, relating the latter to the former in such a way that a difference in velocity results bearing the same relationship as the difference in velocity between stellar time and solar time, then the vortex created gives rise to a distinct form condensing out of this movement. One stream whirls downwards, and because the other whirls upwards, driving with a greater velocity—the lesser velocity would be that driving downwards—this gives rise through the collision to a greater density, a certain figure or form. This figure—though here only as a schematic diagram—is a silhouette or outline of the human heart.

Thus, through the meeting of the Lucifer stream and the Jehovah stream, it is possible to construct or form the figure of the human heart. It is constructed simply out of conditions in the universe. The sun-movement is an expression of a slower movement which meets a quicker movement, and we are so integrated into the two movements that the silhouette of our heart arises; and on to it the rest of the human form is joined. We see from this what Mysteries are actually hidden in the cosmos, for as soon as we admit we have two astronomies, whose results combine—what is the result? The human heart. The whole outlook of modern natural science is based on the fact that it does not distinguish these two streams from one another. This brings in its train the tragic consequence that we then also have a split between natural phenomena, as observed by Julius Robert Mayer and the 'secondary results' he spoke of. Because people are unable to unite what works together from these two cosmic sources, man's thinking rends the world asunder into two extremes.

Here lies the cosmic aspect of something tremendously significant in regard to our understanding of man and the universe. Unless man can renew, in a way that accords with our modern times, the knowledge contained in the ancient Mysteries of a former time, when man was awaiting Christianity, as I have described in the book *Christianity as Mystical Fact*—unless we can bring this ancient knowledge to life in a modern form, as must be done, all knowledge remains an illusion, for that which comes to expression with such clarity in the human heart is to be found everywhere. All phenomena can be explained through the union of two streams, arising from different sources.

The Mystery of Golgotha within the evolution of our earth, however, is something of a totally different nature from all the rest of earthly evolution; and this we shall never understand unless we begin by learning to understand the cosmos itself.

What I have said today is intended as a preparation or groundwork on which we shall be able to build in our lectures of tomorrow and the day after.

Lecture 15

From the foregoing studies you will have seen how necessary it is to study man in his entirety if we would see how exact a copy he is in every way of the universe as a whole. It is specially important to receive this knowledge not only into our intellect, but also into our feeling and will; for only by regarding man in his totality as born out of the whole universe can a deeper understanding be gained for what Christianity wishes to be for the world. It might easily be objected that, if this is so, we are asking modern humanity to develop a complex understanding of the details of the universe and of man before people can become complete and aware human beings. Yet just reflect that this demand, which now approaches humanity as a cardinal one, is not peculiar to spiritual science. In order to show exactly what I mean, let me first ask: What demand did Christianity bring when it first came into the world? In reality it asked for a very widespread understanding of the universe, one which could be traced back to ancient heathen conceptions, but which has in course of time been completely forgotten. Just consider what has been gradually lost to man, in course of time, of the funda-mental views and characteristics of Christianity. Christianity first appeared in such a way that it could only be understood by comprehending the nature of the Trinity for instance: God the Father, God the Son—that is, Jesus Christ—and the Spirit. The manner in which Christianity understood these three aspects of the divine spiritual required an understanding of them no less demanding than that needed for such things as are given by spiritual science today. But all that leads to comprehension of this idea of Father, Son and Spirit has been gradually eliminated; it has been thrown out of an intelligible realm and become empty words; empty husks of words have alone been retained. For centuries man has had these empty word-husks. This has gone so far that, after having first dogmatically rejected them, people have begun to ridicule them. The best of men have ridiculed these empty husks. Ridicule has been poured upon them. 'Dogmatic theology,' it is said, 'claims that One is Three and Three One!' It is indeed a terrible delusion, it is sheer deception to believe that the Christian movement has ever demanded less understanding, less self-sacrificing knowledge, than that demanded by modern spiritual science—and demanded by it in order to regain Christianity. The most important and basic facts have been cast out of Christianity, and if we leave out of account that these live on in the different confessions as words, we can ask what really remains to us of the fundamental ideas of Christ himself? How does modern man discriminate between Christ and the universal cosmic God who can be found in the concept of Jahveh or Jehovah? I have drawn attention to the fact that even theologians such as Harnack do not discriminate. How many people today are clear about what the spirit or Holy Spirit means? People have become so 'abstracted', satisfied with the mere empty husks of words; either they remain in the churches and are satisfied or if they are—as they call it—'enlightened' they ridicule everything. What is given in empty husks of words can never have the power to cast light on the various realms of human knowledge.

Only reflect how far we have actually gone in this direction. In ancient Greece all knowledge at the same time contained a healing principle. The healer was a priest and at the same time the teacher of the people. That the teacher and priest was also a healer presupposes that something unhealthy was present in the whole process of civilization; otherwise there would be no grounds for speaking of a healer. They spoke of the healer because their instinctive knowledge still gave them an understanding of the whole cosmic process, more comprehensive and intense than we possess today. Today man pictures the cosmic process as running its course in such a way that what comes later is always the effect of what was earlier; but this is not so in reality. An older instinctual knowledge was aware that this was not so. Today people, especially those who speak of progress in the abstract, imagine that evolution is bound continually to ascend. We find this notion of an ascending evolution among the superficial philosophers of modern times. Someone who is simply carried along by the general prejudices of the time, such as Wilhelm Wundt, the non-philosopher, who has become the flavour of the month for many, also spoke as a supposed philosopher of such 'universal progress', without the slightest knowledge of what the stream of human evolution really involves. We must realize that in the real stream of human evolution there is always a tendency to degenerate. There is no tendency towards progress there, least of all in history. There is a continual tendency, instead, towards degeneration; and only because what we call teaching, or knowledge, works steadily against it, is that raised up which would otherwise be drawn down into the depths. Only in this way do we progress.

Consider the child from this standpoint. The child is born. People speak of heredity, but we inherit only what would lead to decline. If the child were not educated by his whole environment and later by school and by life, he would degenerate. Education is a preservative from degeneration, it brings healing. The old instinctive knowledge of man regarded as a healing process everything connected with knowledge, education or priesthood. In olden times the office of the doctor could not be separated from that of the priest, they were one and the same. Modern evolution has separated natural science from the science of soul and spirit, as I explained in yesterday's lecture. Thus man leaves to medical science the healing of all that according to Julius Robert Mayer has nothing to do with human aims, but is concerned only with the use of the energy of the horses and its trans-mutation to heat in the horses, in the wagon-axles, in the streets on which the wheels ran, and so forth. This is, roughly speaking, left to the physician; and people like Rubner in Berlin, who is only a representative of this mode of thought, calculate what is necessary to human life almost as though man were a kind of complicated stove.

But now draw the social-ethical conclusion of such a view, and recognize that if, of all that takes place in the trans-mutation of energy, the purposes and aims of man are only a secondary effect, then we are confronted with the possibility of believing that the world could get on without these secondary effects. As a matter of fact that is really the secret belief of modern man, that the real consists only of the phy-sical, and everything else is an 'after-thought', a secondary effect.

In face of such a view it would be only consistent to reject Christianity, as the materialists of the middle of the nine-teenth century did. They actually carried the materialistic outlook to its logical conclusion by saying: If materialism is correct, then there is nothing for it but to ridicule the idea of any difference between a transgressor and a good man—for of course, just the same amount of energy is transmuted into heat in the one as in the other! The questions that flash up in the world at the present time are really often questions of honesty, courage and consistency. At a time when people do not possess this honesty in relation to the outer things of life, it is hardly surprising to find that it is lacking when we come to these cardinal questions.

Thus it comes about that modern humanity still talks of Christ, without really knowing that he must be distinguished from the universal God underlying all nature. If the Christ concept has been gradually changed into the simple God-concept, that signifies a retrogression of humanity, back to *before* the Mystery of Golgotha. In order to understand Christianity rightly it is necessary to take this principle of degeneration seriously, and place in opposition to it the necessity of working out of something quite different from what bears the germ of degeneration within it. The attention of modern man must be drawn to the fact that at that time when the earth was moving—together with man, of course—towards the Mystery of Golgotha, an event took place on earth which had significance not merely for humanity, but for all life on earth.

To comprehend this, nature and spirit must of course be studied far more intensively than people tend to do today. In order to explain this, let me point back to something which lived in the consciousness of man, perhaps up to the eighth century before Christ. Man did not then perceive himself as an isolated being, as he does nowadays. Today he feels him-self as a being enclosed in his skin, but up to the seventh or eighth century BC he felt himself to be a member of the whole universe, participating in the whole universe. Grotesque as it may seem now, it is a fact that in those olden times man did not feel his head so strongly enclosed by his skull, he felt that what lived in his head extended into the cosmos, and belonged to the whole starry heavens. Strange as it seems today, he felt himself in the sphere of the stars, for he felt his head in living connection with them. Thus he said to himself: 'When the night-sky arches over me, it is really I *myself* dwelling there in my head's living communion with the stars.' And he said to himself: 'When after the night the day appears, then the stars which rose on the one side set on the other; and in their place the sun rises. The configuration of the stars then no longer works in my head, for the sun takes the place of the starry heavens, and then my eyes are subject to the sun.' And because he vividly felt: 'My eyes are subject to the sun when I am busy on earth during the day,' he said to himself: 'Just as now, in this earthly existence, my eyes are subject to the sun, so in the existence preceding the Earth* (we call it the Moon stage) my whole head was a kind of eye; not as now, perceiving objects in a twofold way, but, looking out into the cosmos. Then there were within me, in my brain, as many little eyes as there are stars. Out of these little eyes has grown all that lives now in my brain; and my sense-eyes are but later products, subject to the sun as was my brain to the starry heavens. Therefore my brain has evolved from an eye, or really from many separate eyes, as many in number as the stars shining out there in the night. Thus my brain has grown out of a sense organ; and the eye which I now have in my earthly existence, through which I am in communication with my earthly environment, will be an inner organ, as is now my brain, when Earth evolution has been replaced by another planet (which as you know we call the Jupiter-condition). What is now on my outer surface will draw into my inner being. People will then look different. What they now have as senses corresponding with their environment will form an inner organ in future times.' Ancient humanity felt this instinctively and said: 'Light penetrates through the eye of my senses, but in my inner being I preserve the light of olden times. It works in me as thought. Thought was a sense-perception before the earth entered on the Earth stage of evolution, when it was an earlier planet; and my sense-perception will be thought in the future.' In ancient times man perceived all this as wisdom, which he felt 'instinctively' as we should say today. The ancients did not throw about the word 'instinctive' as is done today, they said: 'It is the wisdom which the Gods in heaven have brought down to us on earth.'

---

* In the following passage, as elsewhere in the book, initial capitals are used where an evolutionary stage of our planet is indicated, rather than a celestial body or planet as it is at present.

Of what arose in them instinctively concerning the past, present and future, they said: 'This was brought to us by the Immortals.' This they represented to themselves in *pictures*. What does the Isis-picture tell us? 'I am the All; I am the past, the present and the future. No mortal has ever lifted my veil.' The modern interpretation of this is really a strange one! People today think in materialistic terms about anything containing the term 'mortal'. They do not think, in the case of this saying of Isis: 'I am the past, I am the present, I am the future. No *mortal* has yet lifted my veil'; but they think of it as: 'I am the past, the present and the future; no *man* has yet lifted my veil.' People of today do not reflect how, on the other hand, they hold themselves to be immortal and that therefore 'No mortal has ever ever lifted my veil' cannot be regarded as an ultimate conclusion. Novalis said: 'Well then, we must become immortal, so that we may lift the veil of Isis.'

Let us reflect on the underlying thought which modern materialistic humanity has produced. It takes some pleasure in this idea of 'I am the All. I am the past, the present and the future. No man has yet lifted my veil' for man is thus spared the effort of lifting it, and philosophers can teach that man has now reached the boundaries of knowledge. In reality they mean that man is too indolent to tread the path of knowledge. They do not like to say this, so they say that man has reached the boundaries of knowledge, beyond which he cannot go.

In our age, which wants to be free of authority, these things are accepted, but they must not be carried into the future, if man is to avoid decadence. It should not be overlooked that no one has the right to call himself a Christian who believes only in a general idea of progress and does not realize that if the earth had been left to itself since the Mystery of Golgotha it would have fallen into decadence. Hence it is necessary for us to oppose this decadence with something which we *cannot* obtain from the earth, nor from what the earth derives from— the Father God—but which must be obtained from God the

Son, and must be infused into the ongoing course of our evolution. To continually refuse to acknowledge the connection between the universe and the Christ event is to turn man aside from his present task. Think what it really means when, though attacked by Catholic and Evangelical confessions, spiritual science asserts that the Christ-concept and the cosmos-concept must be united. 'Spiritual science,' says these confessions, 'has no idea that Christ is only to be understood in an ethical sense, as something relating only to the moral order of the world.' If man believes the moral world order to be a secondary effect of the transmutation of energy, then the Christ-concept relating only to this moral order also appears as a mere secondary effect in the cosmic system.

We have spoken of one thing which an ancient instinctive knowledge of mankind was aware of, namely, that the human brain stands in relation to the starry sphere, and that the human eyes are in a certain way ascribed and subject to the sun-sphere. Going back into earlier periods, when man still possessed a qualitative knowledge of astronomy and of the earthly elements, we see that light was brought into relation with what is nearest our earth, with air. With their instinctive knowledge, the ancients could not think of light without air. Modern thinkers with their abstract knowledge do not bring what they explain as light into relation with air. Certainly they describe it in a wonderful way—as a vibratory movement of the ether; but in relation to air, the farthest they go is to regard the air as a medium through which light passes. It is really most remarkable how little people reflect upon what is simply held up as truth! Earth, infinite space, stars. Among these stars are some whose light needs millions of years to reach the earth. Night falls. Here is a star whose light needs a shorter time to reach the earth. Just imagine for a moment: what do we have in the rays of its light? Certainly we do not see the star itself when we look in the direction of the light-rays. The light-ray which meets our eye, according to this theory, comes from something millions of years back; the source of light may even have perished long ago, but its light is still travelling to us. Nothing is told us of what is really out there in the cosmos. All we are told is how light waves are approaching, which may perhaps come from some still existing star but which may also come from some star no longer there.

We must acquaint ourselves with the way in which light-phenomena as such appear to us in the phenomenon of air; for although light passes through apparently airless space, we do not see it in airless space, but only in air-filled space, for only in such can we exist. Thus we experience light and air together. In this way we can descend more deeply into the human constitution; we can go a step deeper through, as it were, living simultaneously in light and air. In the human head we can pass from the eyes to the nose. The nose (and oriental philosophy knows a great deal about this), the nose is the organ through which one breathes in and breathes out. The eye is the receptive organ for light. The nose and eye are separated. The nose is adapted to the air, and all that is adapted to the air extends out to the world of the planets. The sun begins things by working on our eye; but everything else works on the rest of our constitution. And as we come down from the starry world into that of the sun and planets we arrive, in the case of man, as it were, at the nose. Then we come right down to the earthly, passing from the nose to the mouth, to the organ of taste, and, taking up the substances of the earth through that organ, we descend from the planetary into the earth-world. We have the rest of man as an appendage—the head as appendage of the eyes, the breast as appendage of the nose, and all the rest of us, our limbs and metabolism, as appendage of the organ of taste. Thus we can apportion man, taking him in his totality to the starry world, the solar and planetary world, and the earth-world. We have placed him into the whole universe, and when we look at his brain—inwardly, not outwardly; not by physical anatomy, but by inner knowledge—we see in the human head, inasmuch as it is the bearer of the brain, a direct reflection of the starry world. We see in all that extends from the nose to the lungs a copy of the planetary system with the sun. If we then consider the remainder, we see that part of man which is earth-bound, as are animals. In this way only do we arrive at the true parallel between man and the rest of the world. Thus should man be understood, right down to the smallest details.

Consider for a moment the circulation of the blood. The blood, transformed by outer air, enters the left auricle, passes into the left ventricle, and from there branches off through the aorta into the organism. We can say that blood passes from the lungs to the heart, and from there into the rest of the organism, also to the head. But in passing through the organism the blood takes up nourishment, which contains all that is dependent on the earth. All that the digestive apparatus introduces into the circulation of the blood is earthly. What is introduced through the breathing, when we bring oxygen into the blood-flow, is planetary. And then we have the blood-circulation that goes to the head, to everything composing the head. Just as respiration of the lungs with its absorption of oxygen, and giving out of carbon dioxide, belongs to the planetary system, just as what is introduced through the digestive system belongs to the earth, so that smaller part of circulatory flow that branches off above belongs to the starry world. It is, as it were, drawn away from the aorta and then streams back and unites with the blood streaming back from the rest of the organism, so that they flow together back to the heart. The circulation which branches off above says, as it were, to the whole of the rest of the circulation: 'I do not share either in the oxygenating process nor in the digestive process, but I separate myself out. I invert myself upwards.' That belongs to the starry world. And the nervous system might be examined in a similar way.

One arrives at no true understanding of man by studying

his physical, sense-perceptible aspect only. In so doing we only find in the cranium that porridge described by physical anatomy! What anatomy describes is worthless in itself. It is in reality the confluence of forces of the starry heavens. To describe the physical brain by itself is like describing a rose by itself. That has no sense, for a rose is no separate, isolated entity. It cannot be dissociated from its bush. It is nothing in isolation from its bush. So too, the human brain is nothing in isolation from the starry heavens.

Let us however here recall the true nature of the sun. Again and again I have emphasized how astonished the physicists would be if they could fit out an airship (as they would so dearly love to), and journey to the sun, imagining they would find there a glowing ball of gas. They would not find this, but a suction-sphere, trying to absorb everything possible into itself, really a vacuum or empty space, nay even less than empty, negative matter. Within the sun there is nothing comparable to our matter. It is not merely empty, but less than empty; it is blank, just like a hole, in comparison with the rest of matter. It is really important that one should not, in these days, speculate on things that do not accord with reality, but fill oneself instead with the spirit of reality. I have recently said a good deal on the Theory of Relativity. You will remember what I said about Einstein's box, which is supposed to refute the theory of gravity. Another claim of Einstein's is that even the dimension of a body is merely relative, and depends on the rapidity of movement. Thus, according to the Einstein theory, if someone moved through space with a certain velocity, he would not retain his bulk but would become as thin as a sheet of paper. This is discussed in all seriousness. Such dwelling in thoughts foreign to reality forms the 'science' of today. And it is the opposite pole to what we have on the other hand as faith.

The physician has been relegated to the purely physical domain, the priest to what is purely of the soul. As for the spiritual, it has been abolished. But when it comes to considering everything beyond the physical as secondary—horses, coach, *these* are real to the physical senses, and the horses' energy, transmuted into heat, heat of the horses, heat of the axles, and heat of the furrows of the road—well, it cannot even be considered a 'fifth wheel' of the wagon, for it is less that that, it is a mere after-thought, a secondary effect. As regards the priest, one cannot even say that he is the fifth wheel of the wagon—for what does he achieve if all the 'rest' is secondary? When doctors such as Julius Robert Mayer make philosophy, it becomes physics; and when the adherents of soul-substance, or whatever it is, make philosophy, it becomes abstract concepts; and the two world-streams flow on side by side quite foreign to one another, the materialistic physician of the middle of the nineteenth century and the preaching pastor; they have really neither understood nor even paid attention to one another, at most perhaps they have contended politically. A time has assuredly now come in which there is but little honesty or consistency, and this state of things must be seriously combated and overcome.

We have not only to combat ill-will, but what perhaps has also to be taken into account, namely, all kinds of stupidity and ignorance. That is how things are. And so, if I may sound a personal note, let me draw your attention especially to the fact that I intend to give three lectures on the philosophy of Thomas Aquinas at Whitsun.* I do not know whether our opponents will attack our right to study Thomas Aquinas here. As you know, an order of Pope Leo XIII declared the doctrine of Thomas Aquinas to be the official philosophy of the Roman Catholic Church; and I wonder whether our approach will be described as unlawful propaganda issuing from Dornach! We will wait and see. Let the wind whistle

---

* See *The Redemption of Thinking*, Anthroposophic Press, New York, 1983.

from whatever quarter, we will await it. But perhaps it is well that we should once meet all the talk that comes from that particular direction with a serious study of the teachings of Thomas Aquinas.

Lecture 16

When we try to ascertain man's position within the whole universe, we need to turn our attention not only to space but also to time. Anyone who follows the history of human evolution a little will find that it is a peculiarity of the Oriental conception of the universe to place an emphasis on space—not leaving time wholly disregarded, but placing everything pertaining to space in the foreground. The peculiarity of the Western conception of the universe, in contrast, is to ascribe very special significance to time, and it is precisely this regard for the temporal in human evolution and the universe which must have primary consideration in a right view of the Christ-force. To recognize the full significance of the Christ-force in human evolution on earth, we must be able to place man himself correctly into the whole universe, in a temporal sense. Today's prevalent belief in the law of the conservation of energy, and particularly also that of the conservation of substance, hinders this. The law of the conservation of energy is one which would so place man in the universe that he stands there as a mere product of nature. Attempts have been made to discover the process of transformation through combustion of what man takes in as nourishment, and to find out how the heat of this combustion and the rest of this strength and energy arise in man as transformed forces of food. Such experiments have already been undertaken with students. They bear some resemblance to the following. Someone sees a building, hears that it is a bank, and endeavours by some method to calculate how much money is put into the bank and how much taken out; and finding that the amounts are the same, draws the conclusion that the money has either transformed itself in there or has remained the same, but that there are no officials in the bank at all. This is approximately the logic of the thought that whatever a person has eaten may be rediscovered in the transformed forces of his calefaction, his activity. Here too courage is lacking actually to put to the test the depth of thought underlying these modern principles. One might indeed arrive at many things by testing both the logic and more especially the reality of what we find in modern science.

Now the point is that because of all these unreal and illogical methods of thought nowadays, man is placed in the dilemma in which, as I have already pointed out, we have ideals on the one hand, as secondary effects, and natural phenomena, on the other, with no means of building a bridge between them. At most, such decadent chatterers in the sphere of philosophy as Eucken or Bergson try to talk of natural phenomena in a way which flatters the primitive thinking of people who do not want to deal with anything real or specific, but prefer to lap up the drivel which they are fed by such philosophers. What is of real consequence instead is, first of all, to ask oneself what man bears within him out of all the depths and breadths of the universe. What is there within him that enables him, as part of the universe, to work with his ego in such a way that one can see that what results from his activity is his own? Now of all things of the universe, of all properties of being in the universe, one such property is easier to study than others, if one only sets aside the prejudices of modern science, and that is the element of *heat*.

Certainly it must be said in the first place that even the animal world, and perhaps to some extent the plant world, have heat of their own; but the heat of the higher animal world and of man can be distinguished from other kinds of individual body-heat. And it is necessary to enquire now into what may be called the heat peculiar to *man*. For in this particular heat (leaving aside for the moment that of the animal, although what I am saying does not contradict facts in the animal world; but it would lead us too far to include it in our present observations), in what we possess as our own heat, and in what separates itself off from all other universal warmth as our own warmth organism—we have our inmost corporeality, our inmost bodily field of activity. We are unaware of this because it escapes ordinary observation that the element of *soul* and *spirit* dwelling in us finds its immediate continuation in the effect it has on the heat within us. In speaking of our bodily nature we should really speak of our heat-body. When we see someone before us, we also have an enclosed heat-space before us, which is at a higher temperature than its environment. In this increased temperature lives our soul and spirit element, and the soul and spirit in us is indirectly conveyed, by means of the heat, to our other organs. In this way too, our will comes into being.

The will comes into being through the fact that in the first instance an influence is exerted upon the warmth or heat within us, then in turn on our lung-organization, from there on our fluid-organization, and only then on what is mineral or solid in our organism. Thus the human organization must be represented as follows: the first part to be acted upon is the heat, then through heat air is affected; from there an influence acts upon the water—the fluid-organism—and thence upon our solid-organization. (I have previously mentioned the fact that the solid part of man's organization is the least, for his body consists of more than 75% fluid.) This fact, that we really live and move in our heat or warmth element, is one of the physiological facts which we must keep carefully in mind, for we must not simply regard what forms an enclosed heat-space as though it were just a space of pure uniform heat, having a higher temperature than the environment—no, we must regard it as having *differentiated* parts, warmer and colder. Just as our liver, lungs and so forth, differ from each other, so do the parts of our heat-organism; and this differentiation is continually changing inwardly. It is a constantly moving differentiation; and what in the first instance unites with the activity of the soul and spirit has its being in this inner heat-organization.

Philosophers today say that the effect of the soul and spirit upon the body cannot be perceived, because they imagine an arm as a sort of solid lever appliance; and of course they cannot see how the activity of the soul and spirit, which is conceived of as abstractly as possible, can be transmitted to this solid lever appliance. But one need only fix one's attention on the transition points, where one realm meets another, and we find there how man's organism is organized in harmony with the whole universe. If we study the idea of the human being in a real way, we find that the thinking which asserts itself in our head has very much to do with this inner activity that goes on within conditions of heat and warmth. (This is not quite exact, but the inaccuracy can perhaps only be corrected in the course of time. We must gradually try to get a complete picture, therefore I will begin with a more cursory description.) If we observe this inter-working of thoughts in the heat-space, in the enclosed heat-space, it is evident that something like a co-operation of thought-activity and heat-activity takes place. In what does this consist? Here we come to something which demands very careful consideration.

Taking first the whole of the rest of man, and then his head, we can, of course, trace metabolism from the former to the latter; and the fact that ultimately the head has to do with thinking can be sensed as a direct experience. Yet what really happens here? We will lead up to this gradually, and eventually arrive at a fitting picture of what happens. Let us suppose we have some fluid substance; we bring it to boiling point, then it evaporates, and changes into a more rarefied substance. This same process takes place far more intensely with human thinking, whose effect on metabolism, in the

208 MYSTERY OF THE UNIVERSE

human head is to make all substance fall away like a sediment and be expelled so that nothing remains of it but mere *picture*.

I will now use another image to make things clear. Suppose you have a vessel containing a solution. This you cool down, which is again a heat-process. A sediment collects below, and above remains finer liquid. This is also the case with the human head; only here no substance whatever is collected above, nothing but pictures, all matter is expelled. This is the activity of the human head: it forms what are mere pictures, and expels what is matter. This process, as a matter of fact, takes place in everything that may be called our transition to pure thinking. All material substance that has been active in our inner life falls back into the organism as it were, and pictures alone remain. It is a fact that when we rise to pure thought we live in pictures. Our soul lives in pictures; and these pictures are the remains of all that has gone before. Not the substance, but the pictures remain.

What I have described to you can be followed right into the thoughts themselves, for this process only takes place at the moment when thoughts change into nothing but pictures. At first thoughts live, as it were, in corporeal and embodied form. They are permeated by substance; but as *pictures* they separate themselves out from this substance. If, however, we go to work in a truly spiritually scientific way, we can quite easily distinguish pure thought—sense-free thought that has separated itself out from the material process—from all thoughts belonging to what I have called in these lectures the 'instinctive wisdom of the ancients'.

The nature of this instinctive wisdom of the ancients was such that it did not filter out matter in this way. This filtering away of all matter and substance is a result of human evolution. Although not observed by external physiology, it is a fact that generally—of course generally and approximately—the thinking of earthly humanity *before* the Mystery of Golgotha was always united with matter, and that at the time when the

Mystery of Golgotha intervened in the life and evolution of the earth, humanity had evolved to a point where it could separate out matter from the inner process of thought—matter-free thought became possible.

Please don't think this is unimportant! It is actually one of the most important things of all that man in his evolution has become free from corporeal thinking, that thoughts have changed to pure pictures. Thus we may say that up to the time of the Mystery of Golgotha, bodily pictures lived in man; but after the Mystery of Golgotha, matter-free pictures lived in man. *Before* the Mystery of Golgotha, the universe worked upon man in such a way that he could not attain to pictures free of the body, free of matter. *Since* the Mystery of Golgotha, the universe has, as it were, withdrawn. Man has been transposed to an existence which only takes place in pictures.

The connection man sensed with the universe before the Mystery of Golgotha, he also related to the universe. He related human life on earth to heaven. We can observe this in quite precise terms. In ancient Hebrew culture people were clearly and distinctly conscious that the twelve tribes of old Israel were projections on earth of the constellations of the zodiac. The twelvefoldness of the universe comes to expression in the life of man; and we may say that in those days the life of man was pictured as a consequence of the twelvefoldness of the heavens, of the zodiac. All human beings felt the starry heavens streaming into them; and they felt this above all as a group, as a community of people into whom the starry heavens rayed. In the evolution of Hebrew antiquity we must go back to the time when we are told of the twelve sons of Jacob as the projection on earth of the twelve regions of heaven. Just as, within Hebrew evolution, there was this instreaming of heavenly forces upon man on earth in the dim mists of antiquity, so we find a similar thing in Europe at a later time, since in the different parts of the globe evolution comes about at different times. We must go back to the

Middle Ages and study the legends of King Arthur and his Round Table, those significant Celtic legends. For Central Europe evolved later to the stage reached by the old Hebrews thousands of years before. Central Europe only reached this stage at the time to which the legends of Arthur and his Round Table refer. There was, however, a difference. Hebrew antiquity evolved to the point where this in-streaming from the universe still yielded corporeal or matter-imbued pictures. Then came the point of time when the body withdrew from such pictures, when the pictures had to be given a new substantiality. There was indeed a danger that man's soul-life would pass completely into a life of pictures or images. People did not immediately recognize this danger. Even Descartes was still floundering, and instead of saying: 'I think, therefore I am not,' he said the opposite of the truth: 'I think, therefore I am.' For when we live in pictures, we really *are not!* When we live in mere thoughts, it is the surest sign that we are not. Thoughts must be filled with substantiality. In order that man might not continue to live in mere pictures, in order that inner substantiality might once more exist in the human being, that Being intervened who entered through the Mystery of Golgotha. Hebrew antiquity was the first to meet with this intervention of the central force, which was now to give back reality to the human soul that had become picture. This,

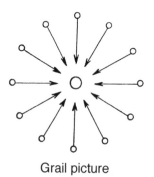

Grail picture

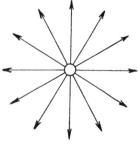

Parsifal figure

however, was not at once understood. In the Middle Ages we have the last echoes of this in the twelve around King Arthur's table; but this was soon replaced by something else—the *Parsifal legend*, which contrasts *one* man with the twelve, one man, who develops twelvefoldness out of his own inner centre or core. Thus in contrast to that first picture (previous page, left diagram), which was essentially the Grail picture, must be set the Parsifal picture (previous page, right diagram), in which what man now possesses within him rays out from the centre. The endeavour of those in the Middle Ages who wished to understand Parsifal, who wished to make the Parsifal striving active in the human soul, was to introduce true substantiality, real inner being into the image-life that could crystallize out in man after all materiality had filtered away. Whereas the Grail legend still shows the in-streaming from without, the Parsifal figure is now set against this, raying out from the centre into mere pictures the inner life that can restore reality to them.

The Parsifal legend thus represented the striving of humanity in the Middle Ages to find the way to the *Christ within*. It represents an instinctive striving to understand what lives as the Christ in the evolution of humanity. If one studies inwardly what was experienced in this figure of Parsifal, and compares it with what is to be found in creeds and faiths, one receives a strong impulse towards what needs to happen today. People are now satisfied with the mere husk of the word 'Christ' and believe that they thus possess Christ, whereas even the theologians themselves do not possess him, but remain at the level of more superficial, external interpretation and exegesis. In the Middle Ages there was still so much direct consciousness left that by comprehending the representative of humanity, Parsifal, people were able to wrest their way upwards to the figure of Christ. If we reflect on this we also gain an impression of man's place in the whole universe. Throughout the world of nature, conversion and transmutation of forces and energy prevails. *In man alone* matter is cast out by pure thought. That matter which is actually cast out of the human being by pure thought is also *annihilated, it passes into nothingness.* In man, therefore, is a place in the universe where matter ceases to exist.

If we reflect upon this, we must think of all earth-existence as follows. Here is the earth, and on the earth, man; into man passes matter. Everywhere else it is transmuted, transformed. In man it is annihilated. The material earth will pass away as matter is gradually destroyed by man. When, some day, all the substance of the earth will have passed through the human organism, being used there for thinking, the earth will cease to be a planetary body. And what man will have gained from this earth will be pictures. These, however, will have a new reality, they will preserve a primal reality. This reality is the one proceeding from the central force which entered human evolution through the Mystery of Golgotha. Looking towards the end of our earth, therefore, what do we see? The end of the earth will come when all its substance is destroyed as described above. Man will then possess pictures of all that has taken place in earthly evolution. At the end of Earth evolution the earth would, without the Mystery of Golgotha, have been absorbed back into the universe, and there would remain merely pictures, without reality. What makes them real, however, is the fact of the Mystery of Golgotha having been there within human evolution giving these pictures inner reality for the life to come. Through the Mystery of Golgotha, a new beginning becomes possible for the earth's future existence.

From this we can see that what is contained in our stream of evolution is not to be regarded merely as a continuous stream, where one thing is always related to another as effect to cause. Instead we must recognize in the first place a pre-Christian evolution, which gave rise to all that people were able to think at that time, for what they were able then to think was contained in the Father God, was imparted to the earth through him. The nature and work of the Father God, however, was such that what he created as Earth evolution was given over to decline and death, to what passes away. A new beginning was made with the Mystery of Golgotha. Of all that went before only pictures were to remain, as it were descriptive paintings of the world. These pictures were, however, to receive new reality through what entered as Being into Earth evolution through the Mystery of Golgotha. That is the cosmic significance of the Mystery of Golgotha; that is what I meant years ago, when I said: Christianity will not be understood until it has penetrated into all our knowledge, right down into the realm of physics, until we understand how, even in physical things, Christ's substantiality works within world-existence. We have not grasped Christianity until we can say to ourselves: Precisely in the domain of heat a change is taking place in man which results in matter being destroyed and a purely picture-existence arising out of the matter; but through the union of the human soul with the Christ-substance this picture-existence becomes a new reality.

If we compare this thought, that of the interweaving of what man has transformed into soul and spirit with physical existence, if we compare this whole conception with the cheerless scientific thoughts of modern times which can only lead us down a blind alley, we shall see its great and deep significance, and we shall see how we should regard laws like those presented by Julius Robert Mayer, which in fact describe what falls away from cosmic existence, even as ice and snow melt before the sun. Man, however, retains the pictures, and they derive a reality for the future because a *new substance* has entered them, the substance which passed through the Mystery of Golgotha.

At the same time this provides the basis for man's idea of freedom and can be linked with scientific thinking—not when we speak of 'conservation of matter and energy', but of the fact that matter and energy have a temporal life allotted to them. We do not participate only in the evolving material universe, but in its decay too, and we are now in the process of raising ourselves out of it to mere picture-existence, and then permeating ourselves with what we can only devote ourselves to in free-will—the Christ Being. For he so stands in human evolution that man's connection with him can only be a *free* one. Anyone who seeks to be compelled to recognize Christ cannot find his Kingdom, he can come only to the universal Father God, who however, in our world, has now only a share in a decaying world, and precisely on account of this decay and decline has sent the Son. A spiritual view of the world must unite with a natural, physical world view, but they must unite *in man*—and through a free deed. Hence we can only say of anyone who wishes to *prove* freedom that he is still adopting an ancient, pagan point of view. All proofs of freedom fail; our task is not to prove freedom, but to take hold of it. We take hold of it when we understand the nature of sense-free thinking. Sense-free thinking however needs to establish a connection with the world again; and it does not find this unless it unites with what has entered the evolution of the world as new substance through the Mystery of Golgotha.

Thus the bridge between a natural and moral world view lies in a right understanding of Christianity. It might at first appear very strange that the very ones who promulgate modern creeds—or rather ancient ones that extend their influence into modern life—do not desire a science leading towards Christianity, but desire a science as materialistic as possible, so that an unscientific faith may hold its own alongside it.

In this sense we can see that modern materialism and reactionary Christianity are very closely related, for the latter has driven mankind into the conception that things spiritual must not be penetrated by true knowledge. Knowledge must be kept free from the spiritual, must be kept away from it, must extend only to the material. Thus on the one hand we have the advocate of one or other creed, who says that science relates only to what is sense-perceptible, and that all else must be grasped by faith alone. On the other hand we have the materialist, who says that science relates only to what is sense-perceptible, and that faith has no place.

Spiritual science is not related to materialism. Modern creeds on the other hand, which are ancient ones in new clothing, are very closely related to it indeed.

I think I have now shown how the possibility of permeating moral law with what we can know of nature, and conversely, of permeating knowledge of nature with moral law, is bound up with spiritual science. For the phantom which external science nowadays presents as man, that illusory picture which shows man as a configuration of mineral substance, simply does not exist. Man is just as much a fluid as a solid organism. He is also an air organism, and above all one of heat. When we come to the level of heat we find the transition to our soul and spirit, for in heat we already encounter the transition from space to time; and the element of soul flows in the temporal. Through heat we pass more and more from space into time, and it becomes possible, by the roundabout way I have touched on here, to seek the moral in the physical. Indeed it might be said that one who thinks short-sightedly will scarcely arrive at the connection of the moral with the physical in human nature—for one can certainly live as a miscreant without any apparent physical repercussions, remaining a well-formed human being. Yet people do not investigate such a person's heat condition, which is changed far more subtly and delicately than is supposed, and works back upon what man carries through death. Today people generally look *upwards* into abstraction, we have our thoughts up there; and we look *down* into the physical-material. But we do not find the transitionary sphere unless we recognize the inwardly stirring heat or warmth lying *between* these, which has, at least for human instinct, a physical as well as a soul aspect. We can develop warmth for our fellows morally—soul-warmth, which is the counterpart of physical warmth. This soul-warmth, however, does not arise through a physical change in the sense of Julius Robert Mayer's theory; it arises—but how does it arise? I might say that here it gives palpable evidence of itself. Why do we speak of 'warm' feelings? Because we feel, we experience, that the feeling we call 'warm' is an image of outer, physical warmth. Warmth percolates into the image. And what is only soul-warmth today will in a future cosmic existence play a physical part, for the Christ impulse will live therein. What today is simply picture-warmth in our world of feeling will live, become physical, when earthly warmth has disappeared, in what is Christ-substance, Christ nature. Let us try to find that delicate connection between external physical warmth and what we instinctively call warmth of feeling; let us try to find it. And then let us go to what Goethe said in his colour theory, in the chapter called 'The material-moral effects of colours', let us see how in his colour-perception he places the cooling colours on one side, and the warming colours on the other; how *he links the material-moral with physical conditions* which can to a certain extent be measured with a thermoscope, and shows how the element of soul interplays with what is external and physical. Then we arrive at one aspect of how a moral view of the world can be linked with a physical one.

The Jesuits of course hate this kind of interplay. Therefore even the best book on Goethe written from the Jesuit perspective is a poisonous book, a terrible book, though much more ingenious and effective than anything written about him elsewhere, because written with inner Jesuitical rhetoric. I refer to the three-volume work on Goethe by Father Baumgartner. It is full of spite and malice, but it is both powerful and effective. We may be very sure that in that world, of which many people have no conception, a world which opposes us too, Goethe is better known than he is among academic circles. Those who appreciate Goethe and bring positive estimation to bear on their understanding of him, form but a small community. There is a large community of those who hate him; we have no conception of how large. Some time ago I pointed out how little awake people are to what lives among us—I once said I would have liked to make a count of all those who knew Weber's *Thirteen Lime Trees*, a work of positive Roman Catholicism. I should like to know how many of us have read it! Very few, I'm sure. Yet soon after publication this work ran through hundreds of editions. Have those who desire to help humanity progress any idea in their waking consciousness of the widespread effect of these things? That they have a widespread effect is certain; and it is through all such things that the struggle against us proceeds. And while we have a small group of Goethe adherents, which is however unable to point to anything of importance from Goethe's wisdom, the Jesuit book on Goethe is written with great cleverness and acumen—a very clever and influential book.

And that is precisely what we need: to be filled with *spirit that is awake*. Spiritual science will surely succeed if a wakeful spiritual life really takes root among us.

Publisher's Note Regarding Rudolf Steiner's Lectures

The lectures and addresses contained in this volume have been translated from the German, which is based on stenographic and other recorded texts that were in most cases never seen or revised by the lecturer. Hence, due to human errors in hearing and transcription, they may contain mistakes and faulty passages. Every effort has been made to ensure that this is not the case. Some of the lectures were given to audiences more familiar with anthroposophy; these are the so-called 'private' or 'members' lectures. Other lectures, like the written works, were intended for the general public. The difference between these, as Rudolf Steiner indicates in his *Autobiography*, is twofold. On the one hand, the lectures given to members of the Anthroposophical Society take for granted a background in and commitment to anthroposophy; in the public lectures this was not the case. At the same time, the members' lectures address the concerns and dilemmas of the members, while the public work speaks directly out of Steiner's own understanding of universal needs. Nevertheless, as Rudolf Steiner stresses: 'Nothing was ever said that was not solely the result of my direct experience of the growing content of anthroposophy. There was never any question of concessions to the prejudices and preferences of the members. Whoever reads these privately printed lectures can take them to represent anthroposophy in the fullest sense. Thus it was possible without hesitation—when the complaints in this direction became too persistent—to depart from the custom of circulating this material "for members only". But it must be borne in mind that faulty passages do occur in these reports not revised by myself.' Earlier in the same chapter, he states: 'Had I been able to correct them [the private lectures], the restriction *for members only* would have been unnecessary from the beginning.'

HARMONY OF THE CREATIVE WORD

The Human Being and the Elemental, Animal, Plant and Mineral Kingdoms

Rudolf Steiner

In one of his most popular lecture courses—formerly published as *Man as Symphony of the Creative Word*—Rudolf Steiner presents an extraordinary panorama of spiritual knowledge centring on the human being. We are the harmony of creation—a microcosm—containing within us 'all the laws and secrets of the world'.

Steiner begins by speaking about our inner relationship to three ancient and sacred representatives of the animal kingdom—eagle, lion and bull—and to the forces of the cosmos that form them. He goes on to deepen these themes by approaching the plant and animal worlds in the context of planetary and cosmic evolution. A new category is then introduced: the elemental nature spirits—the metaphysical beings who work with plants and animals. Steiner gives a unique and intimate description of them and describes the cooperation they offer to mankind. Finally, the human being—the 'harmony of the Creative Word'—is placed at the heart of this spiritual celebration of life.

240pp; £11.95; ISBN 1-85584-098-7

ROSICRUCIAN WISDOM

An Introduction

Rudolf Steiner

The work of Rudolf Steiner is unique in the way it combines esoteric teaching with practical suggestions for the development of social life. Indeed, Steiner is best known today for the application of his ideas in areas such as education, medicine and agriculture. But none of this could have developed without the coherent and profound body of spiritual knowledge which stands at the very core of Steiner's work.

In *Rosicrucian Wisdom*—one of his most complete introductions to modern spirituality—Steiner speaks out of the stream of Rosicrucian teaching. But rather than borrowing old ideas from historical tradition, Steiner presents a wholly new contribution arising from the results of his own experiential research.

He talks of the Rosicrucian path as being appropriate for the modern spiritual seeker, but warns that Rosicrucian teaching should not be taken as abstract theory. Rather than remaining in the head or even the heart, spiritual ideas should reach into daily action, transforming all aspects of life. Steiner goes on to describe many facets of spiritual truth, including the law of destiny, the fact of life after death, ways of developing spiritual vision, humanity's past and future evolution, and much more.

184pp; £10.95; ISBN 1-85584-063-4

FOUNDING A SCIENCE OF THE SPIRIT

Rudolf Steiner

Previously published as *At the Gates of Spiritual Science*, these lectures offer a fine introduction to the whole of Rudolf Steiner's teaching, as well as including valuable material which is not to be found elsewhere. With great clarity and precision, Steiner speaks of the fundamental nature of the human being in relation to the cosmos, the evolution of the Earth, the journey of the soul after death, reincarnation and karma, good and evil, the modern path of meditative training, as well as giving answers to individual questions.

Throughout, Steiner's emphasis is on a *scientific* exposition of spiritual phenomena. As he says in the final lecture: 'the highest knowledge of mundane things is thoroughly compatible with the highest knowledge of spiritual truths.'

168pp; £10.95; ISBN 1-85584-077-4